TO:

From:

100 Best-Loved Bible Stories

Illustrated by Jakob Kramer
Retold by Michael Berghof

English Editor Kenneth Peterson

Designer David Lund Nielsen

Copyright © 2015 Copenhagen Publishing House
Eskildstrupvej 2, DK-2700, Copenhagen, Denmark

www.copenhagenpublishing.com

ISBN 978 87 92105 37 0

Printed in China

100 Best-Loved
Bible Stories

The Old Testament

The New Testament

The Old Testament

For the LORD is a great God, and a great
King above all gods. In his hand are the
deep places of the earth: the strength of the
hills is his also. The sea is his, and he made
it: and his hands formed the dry land.
O come, let us worship and bow down:
let us kneel before the LORD our maker.

Psalm 95:3-6 (KJV)

1. The Story of Creation

In the beginning, before time began, the Bible tells us how God created the world. The earth was an empty and dark place and there was no life or light. In six days, God created the world and everything living on the earth.

The first thing God created was the light. God said, "Let there be light." Suddenly, the first bright light began to shine on the empty, stormy waters covering the earth. God saw the light was good and He named the light "day," and He called the darkness "night."

Now, God commanded the waters covering the whole earth to pull back. God divided the earth between the dry land and the big seas. And so it happened. Now the world had mountains and valleys. It had lakes and rivers.

And God said, "Let the earth be filled with green grass." He put

tall trees and beautiful flowers everywhere. He filled the world with color. And God saw all he created was wonderful and said to himself, "This is good."

On the fourth day, God made the sun, the moon, and the stars. He made the sun shine from the sky during the day and the moon to shine in the night along with all the countless glittering stars of the universe.

But the earth was very quiet and still because no living beings had been created. Then, on the fifth day, God created fish in the seas and rivers, and birds to fly through the sky.

On the sixth day, God made animals of every kind to live on the dry land of the earth. God made every animal you can think of, from elephants and zebra's, lions and cattle, sheep, dogs and cats, to all the smallest creatures you can find on earth. When God had created all this He said, "This is really, really, good."

God was almost finished creating the world. But something important was still missing. God knew the most fantastic of all his creations had not yet been created.

2. Adam and Eve

On the sixth day God said, "I want to create people. They shall have a conscience so they can think, know and love Me, and love each other. I will make them masters of everything I have made so they can take care of all the things I just have created." God took dust from the dry land and he formed Adam, the first man.

God gave Adam his shape and breathed life through his nostrils so Adam became alive and started to breathe like all living things do. Adam opened his eyes and found himself in a wonderful garden, called Eden, which God had created for him.

Adam was so excited about all the many animals which were surrounding him in the Garden of Eden. So he began to give all the animals names to tell them from one another.

But Adam felt lonely, because among all the living beings he did not find any that looked liked him. Adam was the only human on the earth.

God saw that it was not good for Adam to be alone and said, "I will

create a companion for Adam so he will not be alone anymore." So, Adam fell into a deep sleep. God took out one of his ribs and from it he created a companion for Adam, called Eve. When Adam woke up from his deep sleep and opened his eyes he saw this new person. He said, "She shall be called a woman, because she came from man."

God blessed Adam and Eve and

told them to be happy and enjoy all that he had created. God said, "Have children and let them help you in taking care of everything which I have created. I want every corner of the earth to be full of life and want everything to prosper, blossom and grow. You can eat of everything you find in the garden I have made for you. But do not eat the fruit of the tree of knowledge. If you do so, you will die."

After these first six days when time had just begun and God had created everything, he said, "Everything is perfect now. This is very very good."

3. The Fall

It looked as if nothing could destroy the happiness Adam and Eve experienced in the Garden of Eden where God had created everything so wonderful and perfect. But one day when Eve was standing near the tree of knowledge, looking at the fruit she could not eat, she heard the voice of a creature named Satan.

Satan could make himself look like any animal and he now looked like a snake and said to Eve, "Has God really told you not to eat of the fruit of the tree? Are you really sure God meant what he said?"

"Yes, I am sure God has said we cannot eat from this fruit," Eve said. "But are you sure you cannot just have a little bite of the fruit? I can tell you they really taste good" Satan tempted.

And Eve could not stand the temptation. She reached out and took fruit from the tree, tasted it and she ate it.

She also gave some of it to Adam and he ate it, too. But as soon as they had eaten from the fruit they felt bad.

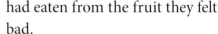

Everything was suddenly different and they were ashamed for what they had done. They also realized that they were naked and were hiding in shame.

In the evening when God came walking through the garden, Adam and Eve dared not to go out and meet him. So God was calling out, "Adam, where are you?"

"Here I am," said Adam and God could hear how Adam's voice had completely changed.

And God said, "So, did you eat from the fruit I had forbidden you to eat?"

"Actually, it was Eve, the woman you gave to me. She made me eat the fruit," Adam said. And Eve said, "No, it was the evil snake that tempted me and made me eat from the tree."

But God was angry and said, "I have told you very often not to eat from this fruit and this means you cannot be here in the garden any longer. Now I have to throw you out of the Garden of Eden forever and you will have to live on the earth where you must take care of yourself. And you will no longer be able to speak with me face to face like you have done here in Eden."

It was a very sad day when Adam and Eve had to leave the garden. An Angel holding a flaming sword was guarding the entrance to Eden preventing anybody ever to enter into the garden again. The paradise in the garden with God was lost for Adam and Eve. But God still loved Adam and Eve. God did not forget them.

4. Noah's Big Boat

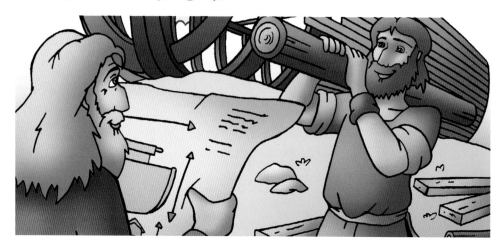

Many years went by and the earth was now full of people. But people had completely forgotten all about God and did more and more evil things to one another. This made God very sad and he tried to find a good person somewhere on earth. God searched, but he found only one good man. His name was Noah. Noah loved and obeyed God.

God said to Noah, "I regret that I created people and I want to start all over again. I am going to send a big flood over the world, but you and your family will be safe."

God then told Noah to build a giant boat called an ark. It was big enough to hold Noah's family and one pair, a male and female, of all living animals in the world. "The ark will protect you and the animals and keep you safe from the flood," God said.

Noah and his three sons, Shem, Ham and Japheth, spent many years building the ark. The ark was built exactly following the instructions God had given to Noah.

5. The Flood

When the ark was finished, God sent every kind of animal to Noah. Two by two they all entered into the ark where rooms were prepared for them to stay. When all the many animals had entered into the ark, God himself closed the big door to the ark right behind Noah.

Then it started to rain. First, water covered the streets and fields and the rain continued to fall all over the world. Then it covered houses and towns. More rain fell, and the ark began to float quietly and safe. The big boat started to float by the wind and the strong current which led the ark away on the big waters that now covered the whole world. But every one inside the ark was safe because God had told Noah how to build the ark to stay dry and safe. Rain kept falling for forty days and nights, and even the mountaintops were covered with water. Noah and his family were now the only people still alive on earth. But God had not forgotten Noah, his family and all the animals in the ark.

6. The Rainbow

Genesis 6-9

After the rain stopped, the ark floated around on the waters almost half a year. The water had dried up little by little and the mountaintops were now visible again. But all the valleys and big forests were still covered by waters. Then one day the ark touched dry ground on the side of a mountain, called Ararat.

Noah opened a window in the ark and sent out a black raven. He let the bird fly away but it immediately returned to Noah because it did not find any dry land. Then Noah sent out a dove to see if the water had dried up from the land. But the dove also returned to the ark, because it found no place to land. Noah waited seven more days and sent the dove out again. This time the bird came back with a green twig in its beak. Noah smiled.

He knew that it was possible to find dry land.

A week later Noah released the dove once more. But this time the dove did not return and Noah knew it was time to leave the ark. God then said, "Everybody can leave the ark, for the flooding is over." And Noah sent out all the animals. They were excited to go out into a new world just waiting for them.

Noah built an altar to worship God and to thank him for keeping his family and all the animals safe. Then God blessed Noah and his sons and said, "I am making a promise to you today. Watch the rainbow I have put up in the sky. This shall be a sign to you that I will never destroy the world again with a flood."

Still, in the time right after the flooding Noah and his family always were a little anxious when dark skies and heavy rain came. But they always remembered God's promise to them and after the rain, when the sun was breaking through, the bright colorful rainbow showed up in the sky. They were safe and God would keep his promise. Always!

7. The Big Tower

After the flooding the world was again full of people. Everybody was speaking the same language and therefore people from all over the world could speak and easily understand each other. One day many people gathered in a city and they said, "Let us build a tall building that will reach to heaven. Then, we will always be remembered in the future as the greatest and most magnificent people who ever have lived on the earth."

But God did not want them to build the tower. He could see how they were only seeking to build the tower because of their own desires to look important in their own eyes. So God came and stopped them by

giving all of the people new languages. Everybody was very confused because they suddenly did not understand what each other said. They could not work together anymore, not understanding what one another said and had to give up their plans. The tower was never completed.

8. God Chooses Abraham

Genesis 12-23

In the city of Ur, there lived a very good man named, Abraham. He was one of the world's richest men and was so rich that he needed hundreds of workers to take care of all his cattle, sheep and camels.

One day God said to Abraham, "I want you and your wife Sarah to move to another country, called Canaan. I have a special plan for you and your family." Immediately, Abraham and Sarah obeyed and began a very long journey to their new homeland. All their workers also had to follow them taking care of all their animals and belongings.

They traveled many years settling in different places before they finally reached the land of Canaan that God had promised to Abraham. They put up their tents near the big trees at a place called Hebron.

9. "Laughter"

Abraham loved Sarah very much. But Abraham and Sarah were sad, because they had no children and Sarah was now growing older. But one night God gave Abraham a new promise and he said, "Abraham, look up at the sky and see if you can count all the stars there are? I promise you that your family will also be too big to count. And your family will give the world something wonderful." Though it was hard to believe, because

Sarah was too old to have a baby, Abraham trusted God to keep his promise.

One day, Abraham was sitting outside his tent at the hottest time of the day, he looked up and saw three men standing close by. Abraham was a generous person and loved to have guests for dinner. So he asked them, "Would you like something to eat?" Sarah made them a very nice dinner and as they sat there and had dinner together, they suddenly said something very strange to Abraham. "Next year, at this same time, you and your wife Sarah will have a son."

Now Abraham knew these men came from God and he believed what he heard. But Sarah heard this and could not believe it. She laughed to herself and thought, "How can it be possible for me to have a child at my age?" But God heard Sarah laughing and said, "Why did Sarah laugh? Is anything impossible for God?" God kept his promise and gave them a son exactly a year later. Abraham named the boy Isaac, which means "laughter."

10. A Wife for Isaac

When Isaac grew up, Abraham wanted a good wife for him. So Abraham called his most trusted servant and said, "I want you to find a wife for Isaac. Go to see my brother's family back in the country we came from and look for someone to be Isaac's wife." The servant took ten camels and started the long journey.

Finally he reached a city called Nahor where he stopped at a well for water because his animals were thirsty. The servant prayed to God to help him find the right wife for Isaac and he said, "When the women are coming to get water from the well, show me the girl who is the right wife for Isaac. Let it be the woman who is offering me and the camels water to drink." Just then a lovely girl came to the well and her name was Rebekah.

First Rebekah offered water to the servant and then she also helped him give water to the camels. The servant kept looking at Rebekah. Now he knew she would be a good wife for Isaac because God had chosen her.

The servant gave her a ring and two bracelets and the same night he asked Rebekah's father if she could marry Isaac. Rebekah's father said yes, and the next day the servant and Rebekah traveled back to meet Isaac. Rebekah was so excited to meet this young man, Isaac, about who she had heard so many good things.

11. Jacob and Esau

Genesis 25-33

Isaac and Rebekah loved each other and soon they had two sons, called Esau and Jacob. The oldest was Esau. The youngest was Jacob. They were twins but they did not look alike. Esau had long thick hair on his arms and legs. Jacob's skin was fine and smooth. As they grew older, Esau liked to live outdoors and hunt. Jacob enjoyed staying close to home.

Isaac was now very old and one day he called his oldest son, Esau, and said, "Esau, I am an old man and it is time for someone else to lead the family. Take your weapons and go hunting. Bring back some meat and fix me a good meal. After the meal I will bless you and make you the leader of our family."

Rebekah heard this and because she loved Jacob more than Esau, she wanted Jacob to have the blessing instead. She then said to Jacob, "Go quickly and prepare some meat and put on clothes that belong to Esau." She then took hair from a small goat and put the hair on Jacob's arms to make his skin feel like Esau's.

Now, Jacob brought the meat to his father and acted as if he was Esau. When Isaac smelled Jacob's clothes they smelled like Esau. And when the old man felt on Jacob's arms it felt like Esau's arms. So, Isaac was tricked by Jacob and he gave his blessing to Jacob instead of Esau.

Not long after Esau returned from his hunting and said to Isaac,

"Father, I am back and have prepared you a wonderful meal. Now, give me your blessing like you said you would do." But Isaac answered, "Who are you?" And Esau replied, "I am your firstborn son, Esau." Then Isaac and Esau knew that Jacob had tricked them. Esau was angry and said he would

kill his brother. Rebekah heard Esau's threat and warned Jacob, "You must leave now and go and stay with my brother Laban who lives in the land of Karan." So, Jacob had to leave in a hurry, going as fast as he could away from Esau.

12. Jacob's Dream

Jacob took all he could bring with him and went on a long travel to stay and work in another country for his uncle named Laban. One night on his journey he was completely exhausted and had fallen asleep using a flat stone for a pillow.

As he was sleeping, he had a strange dream where he saw a ladder going up into the sky. Angels were going up and down the ladder. God stood at the top of the ladder and

said to Jacob, "I will be with you, protect you and keep you safe. I promise that you will have a family that is too big to count. And your family will give the world something wonderful."

The next morning when Jacob woke up he said, "Now I know for sure that God is with me and wants to bless me." He then took the stone he had used as a pillow and raised it up and poured oil on it. It now marked the spot where God talked to Jacob in a dream.

13. Jacob's Large Family

Finally, Jacob came to Laban's house. Laban was a very rich man and owned hundreds of cows, sheep and goats. Jacob worked for Laban taking care of his animals for twenty years. Jacob also married Laban's two daughters, Rachel and Leah, and had twelve sons all together. Jacob also became a rich man and owned many cows, sheep and goats.

But Jacob wanted to go back to Canaan. He wanted to be with his brother and family again. When Esau learned that Jacob was coming home he sent a message to Jacob. He told Jacob, "I am bringing four hundred men to meet you." Jacob was afraid that Esau was still very angry at him. Jacob therefore sent out servants to bring gifts to Esau hoping he was not angry anymore.

But Esau had forgiven Jacob. The men Esau sent to meet Jacob only came to help him with his animals. When Esau saw Jacob he ran to him and hugged him and kissed him.

And they wept. Though Jacob had tricked Esau and made him very angry, he had forgiven him and was very happy to see his brother again. He wanted the family to be together again.

14. Joseph the Dreamer

Genesis 37-47

Jacob had twelve sons and a daughter. Joseph was his second youngest son and he loved him very very much. Therefore Jacob had a beautiful coat made for Joseph. The coat was expensive and Joseph's special coat made his brothers very jealous.

Joseph had many dreams. One day Joseph dreamed that he and his brothers were cutting stalks of grain. They tied the grain into bundles.

But the brother's bundles all bowed down in front of Joseph's bundle.

Another time Joseph dreamed that he saw the sun, the moon, and twelve stars. One of the stars was named for Joseph and in the dream he saw all the other stars bowed down to his star. When Joseph told his brothers about the dreams he had, they became very angry because they did not like his dreams. They said, "So, do you really think it would be right for us to bow down before you, although you are our younger brother? Dream on, little brother." And from that point they decided they wanted to get rid of Joseph.

One day, when Joseph and his brothers were far from home they

caught him, tore off his coat, and they threw him down into a dried out well. When some businessmen came by, the brothers pulled Joseph up again and sold him to these men as a slave. They were traveling to Egypt where Joseph ended up a slave. But God had not forgotten Joseph and he protected him.

15. From Prisoner to Leader in Egypt

In Egypt, being a slave Joseph soon ended up in prison. One of the other prisoners had worked closely with the king. One night, he had a dream and he told Joseph about it. Joseph knew what it meant. "In the past, you were the king's special servant. Your dream means that you will be his servant again very soon."

Three days later, just as Joseph promised, the man was released and went back to the palace to work for the king again.

Two years went by and Joseph remained in prison. At that time, the king of Egypt had some very strange dreams and they worried him a lot. One night the king dreamed he was standing beside the Nile River. Suddenly, he saw seven fat, healthy cows come out of the river grassing along the bank. Next, seven ugly, skinny cows came out of the river and the skinny cows ate the fat ones. Later he had another dream. He saw seven ears of corn. They were thick and full of grain, all growing on one stalk. But another stalk had seven ears that were dried up and very thin.

Then the thin ears ate the thick ones.

The king really wanted to find out the meaning of his dreams. But then the servant remembered Joseph he had met in prison. Joseph was brought from prison before the king. Joseph immediately understood the

meaning of the dreams and explained them for the king. "You have been dreaming about what will happen soon. The meaning is this: First, Egypt will have seven good years with plenty of food to eat. But then there will be seven very bad years where no food will grow at all."

Joseph also suggested that the king should build large storage buildings and gather all the extra food in the seven good years so he could still feed everyone when the bad years arrived. The king liked Joseph's plan and put him in charge of storing as much food as possible in the good years. Joseph was now a powerful leader in Egypt.

16. Joseph's Brothers in Egypt

Genesis 37-47)

Exactly, like Joseph had explained to the king, Egypt had seven years of good crops and then the bad years came. It was not only in Egypt that the harvests failed, and people from all over the world were starving. Soon, rumors went out that there was food to get in Egypt.

Back in Canaan, Jacob and his sons were also hungry and did not have any food. Therefore, old father Jacob sent his sons to Egypt to buy grain. The brothers did not know it, but it was Joseph, their little brother that they had sold as a slave many years before, they now had to meet with to buy the grain.

When the brothers came before Joseph they bowed down in deep respect. Joseph immediately recognized his brothers—but they could not recognize him as he was dressed up in his royal Egyptian clothes. Joseph did not reveal himself to them and allowed them to buy as much grain they needed.

Not long after that, the brothers had to travel

to Egypt again to buy more grain, and this time they also brought with them the youngest brother, Benjamin at Joseph's request. Once again they all bowed down before Joseph. This was exactly the way Joseph had dreamed it would happen so many years earlier. But this time, Joseph could not keep back his tears when he saw his little brother, Benjamin.

Joseph said to his brothers, "I am Joseph, your brother that you sold as a slave in Egypt. Don't be afraid of me. You did evil to me, but God has turned it into something good."

Then Joseph embraced and kissed his little brother Benjamin and cried out many tears of happiness. He also kissed all his brothers and he said to them, "Go and bring our father to come and stay with us all here in Egypt so we can all live as one big family again." When the king of Egypt heard about Jacob's father and brothers coming, he gave them a wonderful piece of land in Egypt.

17. Moses in the Basket

After Joseph and his family had died, their children, called the Israelites, still lived in Egypt in the land of Goshen. But things did not go well for the Israelites after Joseph died. New kings, called Pharaohs, did not like the Israelites and forced them to live as slaves in Egypt. They had to work hard and long and did not have much food.

The evil Pharaoh was afraid that the Israelites would have so many children that they would outnumber the Egyptians and try to take over their kingdom. He then made a cruel and terrible decision that all the Israelite baby boys must be killed. The Israelites were afraid of the Pharaoh and prayed to God for help.

One Israelite woman gave birth to a baby boy. She wanted to protect him from Pharaoh's soldiers and made a basket that could float like a boat. Then she put the baby in it and sent the basket out on the river Nile. She did not know what to do. It would be up to God to save her baby.

The little boy's sister, Miriam, was hiding and watching the basket floating on the river. She was worried the little basket could not float and would sink into the water. But then Miriam saw Pharaoh's daughter, the princess, coming down to the water for a bath. She saw the basket and found the baby inside. She liked the little boy and said, "I will keep this baby. He will be my son."

But how could she give the little baby food? She started discussing it with the servants around her. Miriam heard this from her hiding place and quickly ran up to the princess and said, "I know a woman that can give the boy food." The princess immediately thanked her for the offer of help and gave the little boy back to his sister. Miriam was happy as she went home with her little brother. The mother could take care of him as long as he was very little. She thanked God for taking care of their little baby so well.

18. Moses and the Burning Bush

Exodus 3

When the boy was big enough he was brought to the princess' palace where he grew up. The princess named the baby Moses. As Moses grew older, he learned that he was an Israelite. Moses was angry to see how his people were living as slaves in Egypt and how badly they were treated, so he tried to help some of his people. When Pharaoh found out about it he got very angry on him and Moses had to escape from Egypt to save his life. He went to another country, where he lived for forty years, taking care of sheep.

One day something happened to Moses that was of great importance for him the rest of his life. As he was out watching his sheep grazing near a mountain he suddenly saw a very strange bush on the mountain. The bush was on fire, but it did not burn up.

Moses climbed up the mountain and walked over to the bush. Just then God called to him from inside the burning bush. God's voice seemed to come from the fire and said, "Don't come closer. Take off your shoes for you are standing on holy ground." Moses was very afraid.

God said to Moses, "Don't be afraid for I am with you. I have seen my people, the Israelites, suffering in Egypt and I have not forgotten them. Tell Pharaoh that the Israelites are My people and I want the people to leave Egypt. Moses, you must lead them out of Egypt." But Moses was afraid to go back to Egypt.

Moses then said to God, "Who am I to go and say this to Pharaoh?

I am just a shepherd, and I cannot lead the Israelites." But God said, "I will keep you safe. Take your staff and use it to perform miracles in Egypt. You will lead them to Canaan to the land that I promised to Abraham. Go now and I will be with you." Moses was still afraid, but he obeyed God and went back to Egypt.

19. The Ten Plagues

Moses went and stood before Pharaoh. Moses said, "God wants his people to leave Egypt." But Pharaoh answered, "No." Instead he sent out a notice in Egypt and commanded that the Israelites had to work even harder.

Because Pharaoh did not want to listen, God sent ten plagues over Egypt. First, God turned the water in Egypt into blood. The river and ponds were all filled with blood. No one could find good water to drink. But Pharaoh still would not let the people go.

Then God covered the land with frogs. No one could walk without stepping on a frog. Pharaoh called Moses and said, "I will let your people go. But first, take away the frogs." But just when God made the frogs go away, Pharaoh changed his mind and still would not let the people go.

The third plague God sent was gnats that came out of the ground. Gnats were everywhere and came in big flocks. Then God sent swarms of flies over Egypt. All the houses were filled with flies and they covered everything. It was terrible for the Egyptians, and finally Pharaoh promised Moses that the people could leave if only the flies would go away. But again, just as God made the gnats and flies go away, Pharaoh regretted what he had promised.

Then God said, "All Egypt's farm animals will become sick." And so it happened. Many of the animals even died. But none of the Israelites' animals were sick. The sixth plague was sores. Sores covered the Egyptians' bodies, from the top of their head to the bottom of their feet. People were hurting too much to stand up and had to stay lying in bed. Then God sent a terrible storm over Egypt with huge hailstones that crushed every plant and all

crops on the fields. The hail was so big, it even made holes in the roofs and this hailstorm continued all day long. Still, Pharaoh refused to let the Israelites leave Egypt. God then sent swarms of locusts all over Egypt. A single locust is not a problem, but when they come in swarms of millions it is a terrible plague. They ate every green plant that was still alive after the hailstorm.

Next, God covered Egypt with thick darkness for three days. It was dark even at noon. Still, Pharaoh refused to let the Israelites leave Egypt.

God then said to Moses, "Pharaoh will soon let you go. Therefore, go and tell your people to be ready to leave." On that same night all the first-born boys in Egypt began dying. Even Pharaoh's son died. But among the Israelites, nobody died. This was the tenth plague God sent over Egypt, and by far the worst of them all. That same night Pharaoh called on Moses and said, "I have had enough. Take your people and go." In a hurry the Israelites took everything they owned and they left Egypt.

20. Crossing the Big Sea

Exodus 14

Moses was leading the Israelites out of Egypt. During the day God went ahead of his people in a thick cloud, and during the night he went ahead of them in a flaming fire. That way God could lead them at all times, whether day or night. On their way, came to a big sea called, the Red Sea, where they camped. But, once again Pharaoh regretted his decision and sent out his big armies to bring back the Israelites to Egypt.

The Israelites were very scared because they did not have time to build boats to cross the water so they could escape from the army. Moses told them, "Don't be afraid. God will help us." God then sent a strong wind

that blew so hard that the waters were pulled back and a wide path opened in the sea, right in front of the Israelites. The path led all the way to the other side of the sea. The Israelites could now escape from Pharaoh's army through the sea bringing with them all their animals and belongings, without even getting wet.

When Pharaoh's army reached the seashore they also followed the path through the sea. But just as the army had marched out deep into the sea, the wind that had been keeping the waters back suddenly stopped. The army was trapped in the sea and the whole army was washed away as the waters rushed back. God had saved his people from Pharaoh's army.

21. God's Care for the People

Exodus 16-17

The Israelites were now in a large desert where they journeyed from place to place. It was hot and hard to be in a desert, so the people started to complain to Moses that they did not have enough food. So, God sent food to the people in a special way. Each morning pieces of sweet bread, called Manna, were lying on the ground when they woke up. Later in the afternoon God sent quails into the camp that the Israelites could easily catch and eat.

Everywhere they went, God took care of the people and sent enough Manna from the heavens each morning. But one day, they came to a place where there was no water at all to drink. The people started to complain again to Moses, "Give us something to drink" they said.

Moses prayed to God. And God showed him a large rock and said, "Strike the rock with your staff." Moses did what God had told him to, and immediately water came rushing from the rock. Now the people could drink as much water they wanted. Once again God had helped his people.

22. The Ten Commandments

Exodus 19-20

The Israelites continued their journey in the big desert. One day they arrived at the same mountain where Moses had seen the burning bush. Then they decided to put up all their tents and camp there. As they looked up, a dark cloud covered the mountain. Lightning flashed from the cloud, and loud thunder shook the earth. God was on the mountain.

Moses climbed up the mountain to talk to God. For forty days, Moses stayed on the mountaintop where God talked to him. God gave Moses laws and rules for his people to obey. God himself carved ten of these laws on two large, flat stones. These laws were called the Ten Commandments. The Ten Commandments said:

1. Worship God only 2. Do not worship anyone or anything else. 2. Do not make any idol or picture to worship 3. My name is holy 4. Keep day number seven holy and do your work in six days. 5. Honor your father and mother 6. Do not kill 7. Do not break the promises you make when you marry. 8. Do not steal. 9. Do not tell lies 10. Do not desire anything that belongs to another person

Moses carried the Ten Commandments back to the camp and read them to the people. Moses told the people, "We are going to build a special place to worship God. It will be a large, beautiful tent called the tabernacle." They built the tabernacle in the very middle of the camp. They made colorful curtains for the tent and decorated it with silver and gold. When the tabernacle was finished, a cloud appeared and hovered in the air just above the tabernacle. The cloud showed them that God was with them. Always!

23. Twelve Spies

After many months of travel, the Israelites came to the edge of Canaan, the land God had promised to Abraham, Isaac and Jacob so many years ago. God said to Moses, "Send in some men to see what the country is like." Moses picked twelve men and instructed them to go and find out if the land was a good place and to see if their armies were strong.

After some time the men returned again to the camp. The spies said, "It is a wonderful land but we cannot enter Canaan because the people there are giants and they are mighty warriors." When the people heard these words, they were afraid. They started to complain to Moses, "Why did you lead us out in this desert? We were better off back in Egypt."

But two of the spies, Joshua and Caleb said, "Don't be afraid. God is with us and he will help us!" But the people were still afraid and did not want to listen to them. Then God got angry at the Israelites because they would not trust him to help them and he said, "Because you are afraid and don't trust in Me I will not give you the Promised Land right now. Instead, you will have to stay in the desert for another forty years. Of all you people only two, Caleb and Joshua, will go into the Promised Land because they trusted Me."

24. The Walls of Jericho

Almost forty years later, the time came that God had decided for the people to enter Canaan. Moses was now an old man and he knew he was not going to lead the people into the Promised Land. Instead Moses chose Joshua to become the new leader of the Israelites.

Then they came to the big city of Jericho. A high, thick wall surrounded the city. But Joshua was not worried, because God had already told him how the city would be conquered. Joshua now commanded his army to march around the city every day for the next six days.

Then, on the seventh day, God told the priests leading the army around the city walls to blow their trumpets, and all the people shouted out loud at the same. All at once, the walls of Jericho fell tumbling down and the Israelites easily captured the city.

Finally, after all these many years in the desert the Israelites had gotten their own land. The promise so many years earlier to Abraham had now been fulfilled by God.

25. Gideon and the Wet Wool

Judges 6

Like Moses, Joshua was a good leader of Israel. But after Joshua had died, the Israelites forgot about God. Therefore other nation's armies came into Israel and stole their food and animals. But every time the Israelites asked God for forgiveness and started praying to him again, God would help them. God's way to help was to send men who were skilled warriors of great courage. These great leaders were called judges and one of them was Gideon.

At first, Gideon was afraid of the job God wanted him to do. How could he save Israel from its strong enemies? Gideon said to God, "Show

me that you really want me to be a leader. Give me a sign to prove it to me." Gideon then put a piece of wool on the ground and said to God, "Tonight, while I sleep, make this wool wet with dew. But keep the ground dry." And in the morning when Gideon went out to see the wool it was wet exactly like Gideon had asked for it to be.

But Gideon was still afraid, so the next night he put the wool out again. This time he said to God, "I am very sorry, but I need another sign from you. In the morning let the wool be dry, but cover the ground with dew." When he woke up, the wool was dry, but dew was everywhere on the ground. Now Gideon knew for sure that God wanted him to be a leader and judge in Israel.

26. Gideon's 300 Men

Judges 7

Gideon prepared for war against the Midianites and he went out and gathered as many soldiers as he possibly could. Many thousand men came to be in Gideon's army. But God told Gideon the army was too big and that he would have to send back most of them. Actually, God asked Gideon several times to send away men from his army. Finally, Gideon ended up with a very little force of only 300 men. But God assured Gideon, they would be enough to win the battle.

God had a very smart plan for how only three hundred Israelites would defeat the large army of the Midianites. God explained to Gideon that

each soldier must carry a torch, a clay pot, and a horn. Gideon instructed his men to light their torches, but to cover them with the clay pots to hide the light. In this way, they could sneak into the Midianite camp without being discovered.

Then, on Gideon's signal, every man smashed his clay

pot. The Midianites woke up from their sleep when they heard the loud noise of the trumpets blowing. Gideon had also put men in the hills all around the Midianite camp so when they woke up and saw light on the hilltops and the loud sound of blowing horns it looked as if a very, very large army had surrounded them and there was no way to escape.

The Midianites began running out of their tents to try and get away. But in the darkness, they ran into one another and thought their enemies were already in the camp fighting them. So they started fighting one another in the darkness and the Midianites were destroyed by themselves. In this way God, gave Gideon and his three hundred men a great victory over a much larger army.

27. Samson the Super Strong

Judges 13

When Gideon died, God sent a new judge and leader to Israel. His name was Samson. God told Samson that he must never cut his hair. God said, "If you do not cut your hair, I will make you stronger than any other man living on earth." Samson obeyed God and did not cut his hair. Therefore he had very long hair and a big flowing beard.

As a young man, Samson already proved that he was super strong. Once, he fought a big strong lion

that attacked him. But Samson was so strong that he easily killed the lion with his bare hands.

Israel had many conflicts with its neighbors, especially the Philistines, who caused them many problems. One night, Samson was staying in a city called Gaza. The city was surrounded by a tall, thick wall and it had very big gates for protection.

When the Philistines found out that Samson was in the city, they wanted
to catch him. So they locked the big gates, trying to keep Samson trapped
inside the city walls. But Samson easily tore the gates off of the wall, put
them on his back and carried them away from the city. The Philistines
were shocked to see how strong Samson was.

28. Samson and Delilah

Judges 16

A beautiful woman, named Delilah lived in Gaza, and Samson was very much in love with her. The Philistines threatened Delilah to try and get her to find out why Samson was so strong and tell them his secret. Delilah was afraid of their threats, and begged Samson to tell her his secret. The first couple of times she asked, Samson did not tell her the truth. But the third time, Delilah was crying and she asked Samson to tell her the truth. Samson then said, "If my hair is cut off I will loose my strength and become as weak as any man." When Delilah saw that he had told her everything, she sent word to the rulers of the Philistines, "Come back once more; he has told me everything." So while he was sleeping, Delilah had Samson's hair cut off. Immediately, Samson's strength left him.

Now the Philistines could easily catch Samson and tie him up and throw him in prison. They were afraid he would escape from their prison, so they blinded him by tearing out his eyes. In the prison, Samson was forced to push a big heavy stone to grind grain. But the hair on his head began to grow again after it had been shaved.

29. Samson in Dagon's Temple

Judges 16

One day, the Philistines held a big party in their temple to celebrate their god, Dagon. During the party they had the evil idea to make fun of Samson, so they brought him up from the prison. They shouted, "Bring out Samson to entertain us." Over 3,000 people were gathered, and as they got more and more drunk they also became more and more evil. People were laughing and spitting at blind Samson, who was chained

between the pillars of the building with a hand on each one.

Everybody went on partying, but they had forgotten that much of Samson's hair had grown back in the prison. Samson prayed to God one last time in his life on earth and said, "God, please give me back my powers just this one more time." And God made him strong again. Samson pushed as hard as he could. The big pillars began to break and the roof came crashing down on everyone. Down came the temple on the rulers and all the people in it. Thus Samson killed many more when he died than while he lived. He had led Israel for twenty years.

30. Hannah Wanted to Have a Child

Years later, Samuel became Israel's next great leader. Before Samuel was born, his mother Hannah had long wished to have a child, but she did not have any. She was married to a man named Elkanah. He had two wives: Hannah and Peninnah. Peninnah had children, but Hannah had none. Therefore she was very very sad. Years passed by, and one day she made a promise to God. "If I have a son," she said, "he will be your special servant all of his life."

And God gave her Samuel. When he was able to put on his own clothes, Hannah brought Samuel to a priest named Eli. Eli was an old man and he needed help. He also had two sons but they were busy doing bad things. They did not want to help their old father. Hannah told Eli, "I want Samuel to grow up working here with you. It is a promise I have made to God before Samuel was born and now I want to keep my promise."

Hannah visited Samuel in the temple every year and every year she brought him a new coat. Eli, the priest, loved Samuel dearly and treated him like he was his own son. Eli told Samuel all about God and he also taught him everything about being a servant in God's temple.

31. Samuel, the Boy Who Listened to God!

1 Samuel 1-3

Years went by and Samuel was now twelve years old. One night while Samuel was sleeping in the temple, Samuel heard a voice. The voice was calling his name. "Samuel! Samuel!"

Samuel thought Eli called him from his room and ran to him. "Did you call me?" Samuel asked. But Eli had not called him, so Samuel went back to bed again.

But the voice called a second time. "Samuel! Samuel!" Once more Samuel ran to Eli. And again Eli said, "I did not call you. Go back to bed." Then Samuel heard the voice a third time and again he went to Eli. Now, Eli realized it was not just something Samuel was dreaming. Eli said, "I think God is speaking to you. The next time you hear the voice, say, 'Speak, Lord. I am your servant and I am listening.'"

A little later, Samuel heard the voice and he said, "Speak, Lord, I am your servant. I am ready to listen." From that night on, God often spoke to little Samuel. People soon learned that Samuel talked with God. So more and more people came to Samuel for advice. He became a prophet while he was still just a little boy because God was speaking to him about things to happen. Later, when Samuel was a young man, people were eager for him to be their leader in Israel.

32. King Saul

Samuel was leader in Israel for many years and taught people to follow God. He was a good man and he loved God. But when Samuel was getting older, the Israelites demanded to have a new leader. They did not just want a leader but they wanted to have a real king like many other nations already had their own kings. So they demanded that Samuel find them someone to be king and to lead Israel. Samuel had two sons but they were not honest or fair. So, they could not be trusted.

Instead, Samuel found the king God had chosen. He was an impressive young man named Saul. He was a head taller than anybody and a strong warrior. People really expected he would be a great king for them.

They were especially hoping he could defeat their worst enemy, the Philistines. The Philistines were Israel's fiercest enemy and over and over again they attacked Israel.

In the army of the Philistines was a giant named Goliath, who was over nine feet tall. He made fun of the Israelites and of God.

Every day, Goliath stood near Saul's army and dared anyone to come out and fight him. "Come and fight me if you dare," he shouted. But no one was willing to fight him because he was so big and strong and all Israel's soldiers were afraid of him.

33. David and Goliath

1 Samuel 17

Then one day a young boy named David came to the camp to visit his brothers who were soldiers in the army. David was a shepherd and it was a normal thing for young boys to help their family and take care of the sheep back then in Israel. David could see Goliath and see how everyone was afraid of him. But David was not afraid.

David went up to King Saul and said, "I am not afraid of Goliath and will fight him." But Saul said, "You are just a little boy. How can you fight and defeat the giant?" David replied, "With God's help, I have killed lions and bears who tried to steal my sheep. God will also help me fight Goliath."

When Saul heard these brave words he gave David his own sword and dressed him with the king's helmet and armor. But the helmet and armor were much too heavy for little David to carry. So he gave it back to Saul.

Instead David picked up five smooth stones. He put one stone in

his sling and went up to fight Goliath. David shouted to Goliath, "You are fighting me with you sword, spear and all your strength. But I am fighting with the strength God will give me." Then David ran toward Goliath, swinging the sling around and around.

Then he let the stone fly, and it hit Goliath right above his eyes in the forehead. The giant fell facedown to the ground. David ran up to him and grabbed Goliath's own sword and cut off his head. Goliath was defeated. The Philistines were shocked to see that their giant, Goliath, was defeated by a little boy, and they ran away. But all the soldiers in Israel's army were excited and celebrated how David had just defeated Goliath with God's help. David became a famous hero in Israel.

34. Saul and David

Years later when David was a young man, he became a leader in the army. He won many battles and soon people said, "David is a greater warrior than Saul." These words made Saul very jealous. Secretly he began looking for ways to kill David. One day, while they had dinner together, Saul threw his spear at David.

The spear missed, but David had to run away and hide from Saul. David ran away to the mountains, but Saul followed him with soldiers. He wanted to find and kill David.

One day Saul's men came near the hill where David and his men were already hiding deeper inside a cave in the hill. Saul and his soldiers decided to spend the night at the entrance of the same cave. While they were asleep, David and his men snuck up on them from inside the cave.

Saul had fallen into a deep sleep on the ground, with his spear right beside him. David's men said, "Look! Here is your chance to kill Saul and take over." But David did not want to kill Saul and said, "God made Saul king many years ago. So, it would not be right of me to kill him." Instead David cut off a piece of Saul's coat and snuck away without waking anybody up.

Early the next morning, David stood on top of a hill and called to Saul. He held up the piece of Saul's coat he had cut off and said, "Do you see that I could have killed you last night if I wanted to. But I did not harm you at all and you have nothing to fear from me. So, why are you trying to kill me?" And Saul said, "You are right, David. You have been kind to me and spared my life." Saul and his soldiers then went back home. But in his heart, Saul still hated David.

35. Solomon – The Wise King

1 Kings 2-10

When Saul died people made David their new king. David was a great king and built a great kingdom and defeated Israel's many enemies. He also captured the city of Jerusalem and built his big palace in the city. David was a good king because he followed and listened to God. David was skilled with many things. He was both a great warrior but also a fantastic poet and musician at the same time. David played the harp and wrote many songs about God's love and about trusting God in difficulties we meet in our life.

David's son Solomon became king after David. Solomon was a very wise man because he had prayed for God to give him wisdom so he could be a good king and rule wisely. Solomon was so wise that even people from many other countries

heard of his wisdom and came from far away places to meet him and listen to him.

God also made Solomon very rich and he had more wealth than any other king who ever ruled in Israel. But Solomon did not just spend his wealth on himself. He also used his wealth to build the first temple in the city of Jerusalem. This was a very special temple in Israel and very expensive to build. Everything in it was covered with gold and silver and sparkling jewels. Even the furniture was made of gold. When the temple was finished, there was a big party that lasted for seven days during which Solomon officially opened the temple. These were truly blessed times for Israel.

36. Elijah – Fed By Birds

After King Solomon came many very bad kings in Israel who did not care about God at all. Instead, they built all kinds of idols made of rock and wood. One of the worst kings was Ahab. He decided that everybody should worship a god named Baal. Almost everyone obeyed the king, because King Ahab had declared that anyone who did not quit worshiping God would be killed.

But seven thousand people in Israel still believed in the true God, and one of them was a prophet named Elijah. God told Elijah that he had to go and tell King Ahab that they should begin to obey God and stop worshiping Baal. But Ahab did not want to listen to Elijah, and that made God very angry.

So, God punished King Ahab and Israel by not letting rain fall in Israel for a very long time. It was very difficult to find anything to eat. King Ahab wanted to kill Elijah because

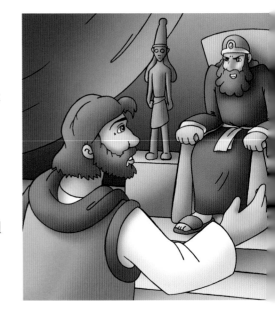

he was God's prophet. But Elijah was safe, far away from King Ahab. He was hiding in a desolate place where no one else lived.

Though everything in the land was now completely dried out because no rain had fallen for months, Elijah was living well by a little stream that still had water. Every morning large birds brought pieces of bread and meat to Elijah so he had more than enough food to eat every day. In this way, God kept Elijah alive with help of the birds he sent as long as he had to hide from the evil king's soldiers.

37. The Big Test

1 Kings 18

Three years went by, but King Ahab continued to be a stubborn and evil person who did not want to follow God. Instead he built more and more idols to Baal. Once again, God sent Elijah to the king and said, "Why do you still worship Baal? Let us now have a contest between the true living God and your Baal who is no god at all. This will prove for good which God is real."

King Ahab agreed to the contest and gathered all the leaders of Israel on a high mountain. The king also brought hundreds of priests who had now started to believe in Baal. Then they built two altars: one for God and one for Baal. They also placed wood on the altars.

Elijah took the wood and said, "Don't set the wood on fire. Instead you can pray to your god Baal. If he is real, he can light the fire on the altar. I will then pray to the living God. Let us then agree that from this day on we will believe in the God who sends fire from the heavens."

Hundreds of priests begged to Baal to light a fire on the altar. But nothing at all happened. Elijah began to taunt them. "Shout louder!" he said. "Surely he is a god! Perhaps he is deep in thought, or busy, or traveling. Maybe he is sleeping and must be awakened." But still, nothing happened. Baal was not God but just a piece of rock, wood and imagination.

38. Fire from Heaven

Now it was Elijah's turn. Surprisingly, Elijah commanded that big jars of water should be poured out all over the altar. He also dug a canal around the altar and filled it with water that spilled over.

Everybody watched closely as Elijah raised his hands and quietly prayed to God. He said, "God, show everyone here today that you are the one and only true God. Let it be known today that you are God in Israel and that I am your servant and have done all these things at your command."

After he had prayed suddenly a huge flame descended from the sky and hit the altar with a loud sound. The flame from the sky burnt up everything on the altar. Even the big stones the altar was built of began to burn and all the water around the altar disappeared as well. Everyone could hardly believe what they had just seen and all fell on their knees and shouted, "God is the true God! God is the true God!"

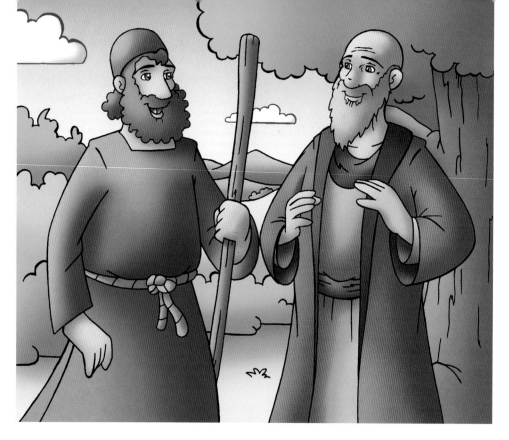

39. Elijah and Elisha

Many years went by and Elijah was getting older and older. Elijah was eager to find someone to replace him as God's prophet when he was no longer living. One day, God led Elijah to a man named Elisha. Like Elijah, Elisha also loved God, listened to and obeyed him. Elisha knew he had been chosen by God to help Elijah. So, the two men became very close friends. Elisha thought that Elijah was the best person he had ever met.

One day Elijah took Elisha out on a very long walk. Elijah knew the day had come for him to leave this world. And God had made a very special plan to take Elijah to heaven. Elisha was very sad when he found out about it. He wanted to follow Elijah wherever he went. So the two men walked further and further away. When they reached the Jordan River, Elijah took off his cloak and hit the water with it. Suddenly, the water in the river pulled back and Elijah and Elisha crossed on dry land.

40. The Chariot of Fire

2 Kings 2

When they had crossed to the other side of the river Elijah said, "I am about to leave you. Before I go, I want to give you something. What do you want?" Elisha replied, "I want to have the kind of power you have." "It is much to wish for," said Elijah. "I will be leaving soon. But if God lets you see me leave, then he is going to give you what you want." They continued walking. But all at once, Elisha saw a chariot of fire pulled by fiery horses coming from the heavens. It came between them and Elijah got into the chariot. Then a giant whirlwind lifted Elijah and the chariot

up into the air and carried him higher and higher until Elisha could not see him anymore.

Elisha looked around and picked up Elijah's cloak that lay on the ground and started to walk back to the river. When he came to the river, he took Elijah's cloak in his hand and hit the water with it, just as Elijah had done. Once more the water pulled back and let him cross on dry ground. Now Elisha knew that he had received the powers God had given to Elijah. From that day on, Elisha became a very trusted and important prophet in Israel like Elijah who had been taken home to be with God.

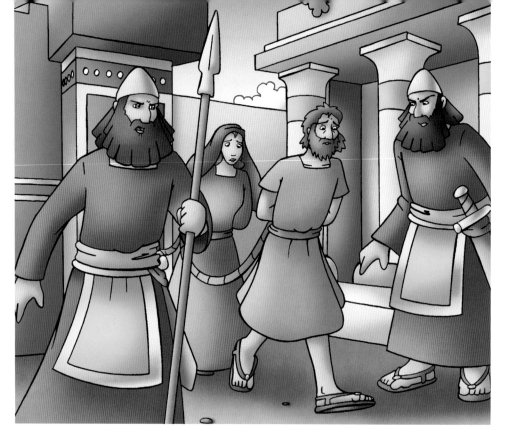

41. Slavery in Babylon

Daniel 1-3

The Israelites were not slaves just once back when they lived in Egypt and Moses led them out through the Red Sea. Hundreds of years later the Israelites were again brought out of Israel to live as slaves in a great kingdom called "Babylon." Israel's many bad and evil kings had forgotten all about God. Therefore, God allowed the king of Babylon to come and destroy Jerusalem with his armies. At the same time, thousands of Israelites were captured and brought to Babylon as slaves.

42. King Nebuchadnezzar's Idol

Daniel 1-3

One of these Israelite men was named Daniel, and he and his friends were going to demonstrate that Israel's God is the true God while they lived as slaves in Babylon. They were put in Babylon's King Nebuchadnezzar's house to work for him. Nebuchadnezzar was one of the most powerful kings Babylon ever had and also a very evil person.

One day King Nebuchadnezzar built a huge idol. King Nebuchadnezzar did not know or care about God. So, instead he had the idol covered with gold and placed it right in the middle of the big city.

Then he commanded everyone to bow down and worship. A message was sent out in the whole city, "As soon as you hear the sound of the horn, flute, zither, lyre, harp, pipes and all kinds of music, you must fall down and worship the image of gold that King Nebuchadnezzar has set up. Whoever does not fall down and worship will immediately be thrown into a blazing furnace."

43. Daniel's Friends in the Burning Fire

Daniel's three friends, Shadrach, Meshach and Abednego did not want to worship the idol which King Nebuchadnezzar had built. Therefore the king became very angry and said, "If you do not worship the idol I will throw you into the fire in the big furnace." The men answered, "God can

save us from the fire. But even if he does not save us, we don't want to worship the idol."

The king turned to his soldiers. "Put more wood on the fire and make the fire in the furnace as hot as you can," he said. The soldiers did what the king said. Never before had the furnace burned so hot. Then they threw the three men down into the fire while the king watched.

But then an amazing thing happened. The fire did not hurt the three friends. It did not even burn their clothes and they began walking around inside the furnace. But now there were four people inside the furnace. The king was horrified when he saw this and said, "I put three people in the fire. But now I see four men in the furnace and one of them looks like an angel."

The king called the men out of the furnace and they calmly walked out. They did not even smell burnt from the fires they had been in. King Nebuchadnezzar knew that God had saved them and realized how strong God is. Therefore, the king decided to send out a new law in the vast country of Babylon demanding that no one must ever say anything bad about the God of Israel. Daniel's friends had trusted in God and he had saved them. Now everybody came to know what God had done on this day all over Babylon.

44. Daniel Did Not Stop Praying!

Daniel 6

Daniel was wise and honest in everything he did, and though he was still a slave he worked closely with the kings in Babylon. The kings liked Daniel very much. But some men in the palace did not like Daniel because they were jealous that the kings trusted him with so much. So they decided to set up a trap for Daniel.

They knew Daniel prayed to God three times every day. So they went to the king and said, "Why don't you make a new law that for the next thirty days, people can only pray to you. Then people can show they are only loyal to you as their king." The king liked this idea and also decided that anyone who was praying to anyone else would be thrown into a lion's den.

But Daniel did not stop praying to God because of this new law. He went home to his upstairs room where the windows opened toward

Jerusalem. Three times a day he got down on his knees and prayed, giving thanks to his God, just as he had done before. But they watched him. They followed him. Therefore, it was very easy to catch him praying to God as he was always kneeling down in his room in prayer three times a day.

45. Daniel and the Lions

The evil men went up to the king and told him that Daniel was breaking the law and had to be thrown to the lions. The king was very, very sad because he liked Daniel so much. But at the same time, he also knew that, being the king, he had to enforce the law.

Soldiers came and arrested Daniel and took him to a den filled with many hungry lions. Then the soldiers threw him down into the den. They were happy to finally get rid of Daniel.

During the night the king could not sleep and he stayed awake all night in his palace. He did not drink or eat anything, and he was thinking all the time about the terrible lions and poor Daniel.

Early in the morning, as soon as the first sunlight came up, the king rushed out to the lions' den. Even though he did not expect an answer he called, "Daniel! Daniel! Are you there?" And Daniel replied, "Yes, my king, I am alive and well. God sent an angel and

it prevented the lions from doing me any harm. God has kept me safe from the lions." The king was very happy and ordered Daniel to be pulled up from the den. Instead he sent out a message to the whole kingdom of Babylon so that everyone would know how God had saved Daniel from the lions. In this way God once more showed people in Babylon that he is the true God that must be worshiped and obeyed.

46. Nehemiah, the Great Leader

The Book of Nehemiah

A new king came to power in Babylon. He was kind to the Israelites who were slaves in Babylon. The king wanted to help rebuild Jerusalem. He also allowed thousands of people to go back to Jerusalem. When they arrived they began to build new houses. They also started building a new temple.

But it was hard work to rebuild the city. After months of work, the people grew tired. Before long, no one was working any more. Back in Babylon the king had a special servant named Nehemiah.

Nehemiah was said because he had heard about what was happening back home in Jerusalem. The workers had quitted building the city because they needed a good leader. When the king heard about these problems he decided to send Nehemiah to Israel. He was going to be the leader in Jerusalem.

The first thing Nehemiah did was to build a thick wall around the city to keep the people safe from their enemies. Everybody liked this plan and so they started to work on the wall.

Nehemiah learned that Israel's enemies planned to attack them before the walls had been finished. Therefore he commanded that every person working on the wall also was given a spear. Though this made it even harder to work on the construction of the wall it only took two months to finish building the walls because God helped them. Jerusalem was now safe. Now, they could begin repair the buildings inside the walls. The city of Jerusalem would once again be beautiful.

47. Esther Made Queen

Esther 2-10

King Xerxes ruled over the mighty empire of Persia. When he needed a wife, his servants searched the land for the most beautiful woman they could find. An Israelite woman named Esther was brought before the king and when he saw Esther, he was very pleased! He was so pleased, he set the royal crown on her head and Esther became the queen. And the king held a big party, Esther's banquet, for all his nobles and officials. He also proclaimed a holiday throughout the provinces and distributed gifts with royal liberality.

A man named Mordecai had adopted Esther as a child. Mordecai was also an Israelite but the king did not know anything about Esther's family background when she became his queen. One day Mordecai went out and sat by the palace gates, and he overheard some men plotting to kill the king. He immediately went to Esther and warned her so she could tell this to the king. The bad men were then arrested, and the king was very grateful to Mordecai for his help.

48. Haman and Mordecai

Esther 2-10

Sometime later, a very powerful man in Persia named Haman became very angry at Mordecai. Haman knew that Mordecai was an Israelite, and therefore, in order to get to Mordecai, he tricked the king into passing a law making it alright to kill all Israelites. But when the king made this terrible law he did not know that Esther, his queen, was an Israelite, because she had never told him so.

Esther was very afraid. But she was also courageous and went to visit the king wearing her most beautiful dress. She wanted to speak to him and ask him to change the decision that Haman had tricked him into making. When the king saw beautiful Queen Esther he said, "What can I do for you, dear Queen? I will give you whatever you ask, up to half my kingdom."

Esther answered, "My dear king. If you really care for me and are willing to help, you can save my people and me. That is what I really want, because Haman has promised a reward to anyone who kills my people, the Israelites."

Now, the king got very angry. He realized how Haman had convinced him to make such a wrong decision. So, instead the king ordered Haman to be hung and the law was revoked. In this way Esther was able to save herself, Mordecai and all of the Israelite people. For this act, Esther became a very famous and respected person in Israel.

49. Jonah's Job

There was a man named Jonah and there was a city called Nineveh. Back then Nineveh was one of the biggest cities in the world, but also one of the most terrible ones to live in because people there were evil and did terrible things to one another. This made God very angry and he said to Jonah, "Go and warn the people in this city that I am going to destroy their city if they don't stop their evil actions."

But Jonah did not want to go to Nineveh, because he was afraid to go and tell them this warning from God. He was afraid of what they would do to him if he gave them this message. Instead he went down to the harbor where all the big ships were to try and get on a boat that was going far away. He just made it as one of the boats was about to leave the harbor to sail across the sea, far, far away. After paying the fare, he went aboard and sailed. So, in this way Jonah tried to run away from God. He tried to flee from God.

50. The Storm

Jonah went down below deck to try and get some sleep. He wanted to try and forget that he actually was escaping from the job God had asked him to do. As the boat was moving smoothly through the waters, Jonah fell asleep.

While he was asleep, God caused a terrible storm to rise over the sea. The sailors woke Jonah up from his deep sleep. Even though these sailors were used to sailing through big storms and tall waves, this storm terrified them. Jonah could see how afraid they were. Immediately, Jonah knew the storm was sent by God and why.

Jonah said to the sailors, "I should never have been on board this ship. It is my fault, because I should have gone to Nineveh, but instead I was trying to escape from God by sailing in the opposite direction. Now, you must throw me into the sea. Then God will make the storm go away."

So they threw Jonah into

the sea. Immediately, the wind quit blowing and the waves became flat. The dark grey sky disappeared and the sun started to shine again. Everything was nice and quiet and the men on the ship were safe.

51. The Big Fish

Jonah was sinking under the water. He went deeper and deeper and deeper into the sea. He saw a big shadow approaching right under him from the depths of the sea. It came closer and closer.

It was a big whale that came and swallowed Jonah alive. It swallowed him in one mouthful. Jonah went all the way down through the belly of the enormous creature.

It was dark and smelled terrible inside. All the time a lot of fish, oysters and crabs that the whale was eating flushed down into the belly of the whale and surrounded Jonah.

Though it was a scary dark place to be inside the belly of the whale deep down below the sea, Jonah knew that God could still hear him. So he started to pray to God. Jonah prayed for three days and nights.

52. Nineveh Is Saved

The Book of Jonah

God had not forgotten Jonah. All this time Jonah was praying to God the whale was swimming toward land. On the third day the fish spit Jonah up on the seashore. Jonah thanked God and then said, "From now on I will always obey what God is telling me to do."

Later, God once again said, "Go to Nineveh and warn them of what I will do." This time Jonah went and warned the people in the city about what would happen if they did not stop their evil actions. The people listened to Jonah and agreed that their lives had been evil. They also asked God to forgive them. When God saw what they did and how they turned from their evil ways, he had compassion and did not bring upon them the destruction he had threatened. Because Jonah finally did what God had told him to do, God could forgive the people in Nineveh, save their lives and not destroy their city.

The New Testament

For God so loved the world, that he gave his
only begotten Son, that whosoever believeth in
him should not perish, but have everlasting life.

John 3:16 (KJV)

53. Mary & Gabriel

Luke 1

A little over two thousand years ago there was a young woman named Mary. God used her in a very special way. She lived in Israel in a small town called Nazareth, and she was planning to marry a man named Joseph. After their wedding they were going to live together in a little house Joseph had built.

One day when Mary was at home, suddenly God's angel, Gabriel, was standing before her in a very strong light which almost looked like fire. The angel Gabriel said, "Mary, you are the happiest of all women. Don't be afraid because God has sent me. I have come to tell you that God wants to bring his Son into the world and you will give birth to his Son. You shall name the boy Jesus."

But Mary did not understand what the angel had just told her and said, "How can this happen? I am not married, so how should I be able to give birth to a child?" The angel answered, "God's power will come over you. And your child will be called the holy Son of God. Nothing is impossible for God, Mary."

Mary was happy that she was going to have a child. But she was also very afraid for what Joseph would say about all of this. Would he believe what Gabriel had said? But God took care of everything. Joseph had a dream in which an angel spoke to him. The angel told him that Mary was going to have a child and that it was by the Holy Spirit that Mary was going to have a son. The angel also told Joseph he must take Mary to be his wife and be the father of her child. So, Joseph obeyed God and he married Mary soon after.

54. Jesus Is Born in Bethlehem

Luke 2

It was time for the baby to be born. But Mary and Joseph had to travel to the town of Bethlehem, over two hundred kilometers away from their home in Nazareth, because it was by order of the Roman Emperor. He wanted to know how many people lived in his kingdom so he could collect taxes from all of them. It was a long and hard journey to travel to Bethlehem, especially for Mary.

When they arrived in Bethlehem they were tired and hungry. Joseph looked for a place to stay, but he could not find one. No one in the town had a room available to rent that they could pay for because they were poor. Instead, Mary and Joseph stayed in a stable, where people kept their animals. It was cold and dark inside the stable, but God wanted them to be, exactly

right there in that humble stable.

It was a silent, dark night in Bethlehem when Mary gave birth to Jesus. Jesus was just as little and helpless as any newborn baby. Mary hugged Jesus and wrapped him in a cloth and laid him in a manger. God's own Son had been born. Not in a fancy palace but in a dark stable. At that moment, no one other than Mary and Joseph knew that God's own Son had just been born that night in Bethlehem.

55. The Shepherds

Luke 2

In the fields near Bethlehem, shepherds were watching their sheep in the night. Suddenly, they saw a bright light in the night sky. Angels were everywhere in the air above them and they were singing wonderful things about what God had done that night in Bethlehem. "Praise God in heaven. Peace on earth to everyone who pleases God." The angels told the shepherds, "A special child has been born tonight in Bethlehem. You will find him in a stable, wrapped in a cloth and laid in a manger."

After the angels had left and gone back to heaven, the shepherds hurried off to Bethlehem and found Mary, Joseph and the little baby. When they saw Jesus, they knew in their hearts that the angels had told them the truth and that it was God's son. They thanked God for the child. They also told Mary everything that the angels had told them out in the fields. Mary kept thinking about all this and she was wondering what it all meant.

56. The Wise Men

Far away, in another country in the East, there lived old and very wise men. They had read more books than anybody else and liked to watch the stars every night. One night they saw a new star in the sky that they had never seen before. The men said to each other, "A new star means that a king has been born in Judah. Come, let us go to Israel and find the new king."

They took their camels and prepared gifts, and then started out on their long journey to the West, towards Israel. They went up to Jerusalem to the palace of King Herod and said, "We know that a new king has been born in Israel because we have seen his star. We have come to kneel down before him and give him our gifts."

But the old evil King Herod answered them, "I don't know where this new born king is. But when you find him, let me know so I also can go and honor this new king." But Herod was lying. He did not want to honor the new king. He wanted to kill Jesus because he was jealous of anyone else who was called king in his country.

The wise men promised King Herod to return and tell him where he could find the new king, and then they continued their search. They came to Bethlehem and there they found Joseph, Mary, and little baby Jesus in a house. Then they kneeled down and honored Jesus and gave their fine and expensive gifts. They were the kind of gifts you typically would give to a king, gold, frankincense, and myrrh.

In a dream the same night, an angel told the wise men that they should not go back and tell King Herod about where they had found Jesus. Instead they went another way back to their country. When the three men did not come back to the palace in Jerusalem, King Herod was angry. He told his soldiers, "Go to Bethlehem and kill every baby you find in the town."

But the soldiers did not find Jesus in Bethlehem. Joseph had also been warned by an angel in a dream about what Herod was going to do. The angel had said, "Joseph, get up and take your family to Egypt. You will be safe there from Herod." That very night, Joseph took Mary and Jesus and went to Egypt. They stayed in Egypt until King Herod was dead. Then they went back to Israel to live in Nazareth where Jesus grew up.

57. Jesus in the Temple

Luke 2:41-51

Around the time Jesus had turned twelve years old, Mary and Joseph brought him for the first time with them on their annual trip up to the beautiful temple in Jerusalem. Every year many people went up to Jerusalem for the Passover celebration and there were big crowds everywhere on the streets around the city. As people walked together they were singing songs about what God had done for Israel in the past. What a wonderful journey up to Jerusalem it was!

When they came to Jerusalem, they went into the temple where the Passover celebration was held. People prayed to God and sang many songs to praise him. Jesus loved to be in the temple with his family and friends. The celebration lasted seven days and then people began to travel back to the cities from which they had come. Joseph and Mary also started back to Nazareth.

They did not see Jesus when they left Jerusalem, but they were sure he was traveling ahead of them with some of their friends. They thought to themselves they would catch up to him further down the road and they

started looking for him as they walked back. But the whole night passed and they still did not see Jesus. Then they became very worried because they realized Jesus was missing. So, they rushed back to Jerusalem to find him.

When they came to Jerusalem they went right into the

temple. And to their relief they saw Jesus as he was sitting right in front of a group of the priests working in the temple. Jesus was listening to them and he asked them many questions. The priests were totally astonished to meet and listen to such a wise boy. It was very clear to them that Jesus, who was only twelve years old, knew much about God. And they wondered how this could be so.

Mary said to Jesus, "We have been so worried about where you were and have looked for you everywhere. Why did you stay here?" But Jesus said, "Why did you look for me? Did you not know that I belong here in my Father's house?" Jesus said this

because he knew God was his real Father. Mary immediately knew Jesus was right and could completely understand why he had not followed them back to Nazareth in the first place. Jesus then left Jerusalem together with Mary and Joseph, and he stayed and grew up in Nazareth until he was a young man.

58. John the Baptist

Mark 1:1-12

"John the Baptist," they called a man who lived far from town, near the Jordan River. Actually, he was Jesus' cousin. He spoke with powerful words and told people to repent from their sins. His clothes were made from camel hair and he wore a wide leather belt. He caught locusts and ate them with honey. "Turn to God and be baptized," John said, "because

God is about to do something wonderful very soon. Get ready. God's messenger will soon be here."

People asked John, "Are you the one who is going to save us as it is promised to us in the Bible? Are you the Messiah?" But John said, "No, I am not him, but I am preparing everything for him."

So, John baptized many people in the Jordan River. This baptism meant a new decision to mark that people were starting a fresh life being honest and trying not to do evil to others anymore. John was standing in the Jordan River every day and he baptized many people who wanted a new start in their life.

59. Jesus' Baptism

One day Jesus came out to the Jordan River where John was baptizing people. Jesus went over to John and asked to be baptized by him. But John said, "Jesus, you don't need to be baptized. It is I who needs to be baptized by you." But Jesus insisted, "I want you to baptize me. This is how it must be." So, John baptized Jesus.

When Jesus came up from the water right after his baptism something fantastic happened. It was as if a gate right into heavens had been opened and the voice of God was heard high in the sky. The voice said, "This is My Son. I love him very much." And it looked as if a white dove was descending down from heaven upon Jesus. This was God's Holy Spirit. John then said, "This is God's great messenger. This is the one I have been telling you about . . . "

After this Jesus went out into a desert place to be alone and to pray to God. Jesus prayed a very long time without eating. Jesus knew he needed God to give him strength to do his important work on earth.

60. "Come And Follow Me"

Mark 1:16-20

After Jesus had been baptized he started to teach people about God and his kingdom. Jesus lived near a large lake called the Sea of Galilee and one day as he came walking by the shore of the lake he saw some fishing boats and some men in them. The fishermen had big nets and used them to catch fish.

These men's names were Peter, Andrew, John and James and they were going to be Jesus' first disciples. Jesus called on them and said, "Come and follow me. And I will teach you how to fish for men." Immediately, the men left their boats and nets and followed Jesus.

Now Jesus already had four friends. They were called disciples, because in a special way they followed Jesus and learned from him so they could later teach Jesus' message to others. Soon after, Jesus met other men and he also called them

to follow him. Not long after Jesus had gathered twelve disciples. The twelve wanted to follow Jesus and they traveled to many places in Israel, everywhere Jesus went for the next three years.

61. The Wedding at Cana

John 2:1-11

Jesus and some of his disciples were invited to a big wedding in Cana. Jesus' mother, Mary, was also invited. It was a really big party and they had the most wonderful food and wine served and there was music and many songs. Everybody was happy and celebrated with the young couple that had just been married.

But during the party Mary came to Jesus and brought some bad news, "I have found out that the wine has run out and they don't have more to serve. Can you help them?" Then Mary went to the servants and told them to do everything Jesus wanted them to do.

There were six big empty jars in the kitchen. Jesus went up to the

servants, pointed at the jars and said, "Fill up these empty jars with water." They did what Jesus said and filled them with pure water. "Now, try and take up some and serve it to the guest," Jesus then said.

The servants took out some of the water from the jars. But it was no longer just water. It

had turned into the most fantastic wine you can think of. Everybody at the party said that this wine was the best they had ever tasted. God had given Jesus the power to do this miracle turning the water into wine. This was only the first of many miracles Jesus was going to do. In his life he did many more miracles to show that Jesus was the Son of God.

62. "Don't Worry About Tomorrow"

Everyone was talking about Jesus. The people loved to hear what Jesus knew about God and still more and more people followed Jesus. Who was he and how could he teach with so much wisdom? One day Jesus was teaching his disciples on the side of a mountain. The crowd had also followed and they sat on the ground close by and listened too. They wanted to hear what Jesus had to say, too.

Jesus said, "Look at the birds. Do they build barns to store their food? No, but God still feeds them. Don't be afraid that you will have no food. Don't be afraid that you will have no clothes. God will take care of you. Ask God for food and ask him for the things you need in order to live. But don't worry about tomorrow. Just ask God for the things you need today."

"And take a look at the flowers. They don't worry about what to wear. Yet, God dresses them in the most fantastic and beautiful colors. To God you are more important than all the birds. And you are more important than every flower on earth." God takes care of the flowers and the birds. He will also take care of you, always!"

123

63. Through the Roof to Jesus

Mark 2:1-12

In every town Jesus entered, he healed many people. Blind were seeing again, deaf people could hear and lame people could walk. Jesus taught people about God everywhere he went. One day he was teaching in a house in Capernaum. The house was filled with people and no one else could get inside the house.

Four men came to the house Jesus was in with a friend who was paralytic. He lay on a stretcher because he could not walk. They knew that Jesus could make their friend walk again. They tried to take their friend inside, but they could not enter the house because the crowd was too big. But they insisted. They wanted to bring their friend to Jesus.

Then they had a smart idea. They climbed up on the roof of the house and carried their friend with them. They tore the roof off of the house and made a hole big enough so they could lower their friend lying on the stretcher down into the room right in front of Jesus. Everybody looked at the man lying on the stretcher.

Jesus was overwhelmed to see the

many efforts of the paralytic man's friends and he looked at the man and said, "Your sins are forgiven." But the people in the house got angry and said, "Only God can forgive sins." Jesus then replied, "You don't believe that I have the power to forgive sins, do you? Well, do you think I have the power to make this man walk?"

And Jesus said to the man, "Stand up! Pick up your stretcher and go home." Immediately, the man jumped up. He picked up his stretcher and walked right through the crowd. The people who saw this were amazed. They said, "We have never seen anything like this before."

64. Two Fish and Five Loaves of Bread

John 6:1-14

Another day, Jesus and his disciples went up in some mountains to spend some time alone. They were far away from town but people had seen Jesus leave and so they also followed him out into the mountains. Still more people came and now over five thousand people had come to hear him teach and ask Jesus to heal their diseases. It was now getting late and everyone was getting very hungry.

The disciples then said, "Jesus, ask the people to leave now so they can go home and get something to eat." But it was a very desolate place and Jesus knew it would take the hungry people many hours to get back home. Jesus then said to the disciples, "Give these people some food," But the disciples said, "We don't have any food and we have no money to buy food for them."

But then they found a little boy. He had brought two fish and five loaves of bread with him. They brought him to Jesus and said, "This little boy has some food and it is all we have found. But it is not enough for all these people." Jesus answered, "Tell the people to sit down on the grass."

Jesus took the food. First he thanked God for it and then he began breaking off pieces of the bread and the fish. He then handed out pieces of bread and fish to the disciples and said, "Give this to the people."

The disciples went through the crowd and passed out pieces of bread and fish. Jesus kept handing the disciples more and more bread and fish. Soon everyone had eaten as much as they wanted. When everybody was full, the disciples gathered twelve more full baskets of the leftovers. In Jesus' hands the little boy's five loaves of bread and two fish fed more than five thousand people on that day. What a fantastic miracle God had done!

65. Jesus Walks On Water

Matthew 14:22-32

Jesus told his disciples that he wanted to go up on a mountain and spend some time alone. He wanted to spend time praying to God. Jesus therefore told the disciples to take a boat and sail across the big lake of Genesareth. He would then meet them again later on the other side of the lake.

When Jesus went up to pray, the disciples set sail in a boat. As they sailed far out on the big lake, suddenly a very strong storm with dark

rainy skies came and hit the boat. Big waves smashed the boat again and again and the disciples were very afraid. They feared the boat would sink.

Just as it looked like all was lost, suddenly, Jesus came walking on the water to meet them. In his white clothes, Jesus looked like a ghost to the disciples and they were even more afraid. But then Jesus called, "Don't be afraid. It is me."

66. Peter and Jesus

Peter wanted to be sure it was Jesus and said, "Jesus, if it is you, tell me to come out of the boat to meet you on the water." "Come, Peter," Jesus said and Peter now clearly recognized Jesus' voice.

Peter stepped out on the water and he walked a little while on the surface of the water just like Jesus. But when he looked away from Jesus and down at the big waves he started to feel the strong winds blowing and was afraid of the dark sea beneath him. Peter started sinking down into the water and he shouted, "Save me, Jesus, help me!"

Immediately, Jesus went over to Peter, grabbed him and pulled him out of the water. "Peter," Jesus said, "Why were you afraid? Why did you not trust me?" Then they went up in the boat and the storm stopped. Having seen all this, Jesus' disciples were astonished. They all said, "Jesus, you are truly God's Son."

67. Jairus' Little Daughter

Luke 8:40-56

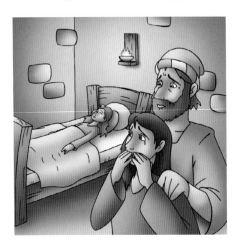

There was a man and woman in Capernaum and they had a daughter. She had just turned twelve years old, but sadly had gotten very ill. The doctors did not know what to do with her. Her father, named Jairus, got very worried and sad. But then he remembered Jesus. Jairus had heard much about him and was hoping Jesus could heal his little daughter.

Jairus rushed out of his house to try and find Jesus. It was easy because, as always, big crowds of people were surrounding Jesus. Jairus pushed and pull himself through the crowd and came and stood right before Jesus. Jairus then pleaded, "Jesus, please will you come to my house and place your hands on my little girl. She is very ill and I know you can heal her." So, Jesus went with Jairus to his house.

Before they reached Jairus' house, a man came running to Jairus and said, "I am so sorry to tell you but your daughter has already died. Now, there is no need for Jesus to come and heal her anymore. She is already dead." But Jesus said to Jairus,

"Don't be afraid. Just trust that I can still help you." And Jairus trusted Jesus and was not sad anymore.

When they arrived at Jairus' house Jesus went straight into the room where the little girl lay in her bed. Everyone in the house was crying and very sad, but Jesus said, "Go outside. She is only sleeping." Then Jesus took the girl's hand and said, "Little girl, I say to you: Get up." Immediately, her heart started beating again and she opened her eyes. She was not dead anymore. Jesus had healed her and brought her back to life. Jairus was overwhelmed with joy for what God had done for him and thanked Jesus.

68. The Good Shepherd
Luke 15:1-7 & John 10:11

Jesus loved to tell stories and people enjoyed listening to them because they always taught important things about who God is and what he is doing. "Listen and try to imagine," Jesus said, "that you were a shepherd taking care of sheep."

The shepherd had one hundred sheep and he took very good care of them. Everyday he led the sheep to fresh green grass and water so they had all they needed. The shepherd knew every one of his sheep so well he could even tell whether they were doing well or if some of them were about to get ill.

As time went by, the sheep learned to stay close to the shepherd because they knew everything would be fine as long as they were in his sight. Every evening when they returned back home, the shepherd carefully counted all his sheep before he locked them behind fences so they were safe from the wild animals for the night. Back then in Israel everybody knew about sheep and shepherds. Therefore Jesus' words made much sense to the people who heard the story. Jesus then said, "I am like this good shepherd and I will lay down my life for my sheep. I know my sheep and my sheep know me."

69. The Sheep That Was Lost

Luke 15:1-7

A shepherd had hundred sheep. But one evening, as the shepherd returned back home, he counted and realized that one sheep was missing. He only counted 99, so he knew a sheep had been lost somewhere. After counting the sheep once more he was sure that it was a little sheep that was missing. It was now getting very dark, but the shepherd was sure that he had to leave the 99 sheep inside the fence and go out to find the missing sheep.

The shepherd went out searching in the dark fields. As the sun was almost below the horizon, he went further and further away from home to find the sheep. Then suddenly he heard the sheep calling and rushed to find it. When he found the sheep, he took it and placed it on the back of his shoulders and carried it back home. The shepherd was very happy because the sheep that had been lost was found again.

Jesus then said, "The meaning of this story

is to explain to you that God is exactly like this good shepherd in the story who loves his sheep. If any human being is lost, God will find and bring him back again no matter what it requires. And just like the good shepherd in the story, God is very happy when he finds someone who has been away from him. Actually, God's joy is much more than the shepherd's. That is because human beings are so much more valuable to God than sheep are."

70. The Farmer and the Seed

Matthew 13:1-23

Jesus once told a very interesting story about a farmer who was planting his crop. With his big bag of seeds he went out in the field and tossed the seed here and there, all over his field. This was the typical way how a farmer would plant his crop back then in Israel. Some of the seed fell on a path where people and animals walked every day. The ground there was hard, so the seed was not able to sink into the ground and grow roots. Not long after, birds came and they ate the seed.

Other seed fell where the ground was filled with stones and only a thin layer of soil. As soon as the sun came the seed started to grow but quickly it was dried out in the heat of the burning sun because the roots could not grow deep enough in the thin layer of soil. Soon the little plants had died.

Still, other seed fell in places covered with weeds and thorns. Here, too, the seed began to grow. But the weeds and the thorns were too thick and were growing faster than the seed. They took all the sunlight and water and the new plants only lasted a few days before they died.

71. The Good Soil

But the rest of the seed fell on good ground with no stones, weeds or thorns in the soil. The plants put down deep roots and they quickly grew big and tall. Not long after they had been planted the farmer had a wonderful harvest from these seeds that fell in the good ground.

When Jesus finished this story, his disciples asked him its meaning. Jesus answered, "This story is really about how people listen to what I have to say. The seeds are my words. The birds, the soil filled with stones, the weeds and thorns are like different

people and how they listen to my words, the seeds. Some don't listen at all because their hearts are hard like the ground along the path. Others listen carefully at first, but then quickly again lose interest. They are like the soil filled with stones. The third kind of people is like the soil with weeds and thorns. They start out being very excited about me. But after a little while, they start to worry about many things. They worry about money and having enough food, and all these worries fill them up so much that their love for God dies."

"Finally, there are those who in their hearts are like the good soil in the story. They listen to what I teach them about God. Therefore God's love grows in their hearts everyday just like a strong plant that grows a little day by day. These people will surely become filled with true joy because they follow and live by my words."

72. The Treasure

Jesus once told two small stories about God's kingdom. If we love God and believe in him we will be living in God's kingdom, even here on earth. Jesus also said that if we begin to really understand God's kingdom it will be like a hidden treasure which is suddenly found. It will completely change a person's life and decisions.

Jesus said, "A man was plowing a field that belonged to someone else. All of a sudden his plow struck something very hard. The man stopped and started digging in the ground to find out what it was. He thought

that it was probably just a big rock and wanted to remove it from the field. But what a surprise!! There in the ground was a box filled with a costly treasure. Quickly the man covered the box again with dirt and hid the treasure he had just found. Then he rushed to town where he sold everything he had ever owned to have enough money to buy the field. He paid the owner of the field everything he had. But now the treasure in the field was his and he was full of joy."

73. The Beautiful Pearl

Matthew 13:44-46

There was a man who bought and sold pearls. He was always looking for pearls that were truly beautiful. Everywhere he went, he always looked for beautiful and expensive pearls that he easily could sell and make a good profit.

But one day, a very special pearl caught his eye. He had never seen a more beautiful and perfect pearl in his whole life. And having worked with buying and selling pearls he had seen a lot…but never anything similar to this pearl! Then he said to himself, "I

must have this one. This pearl will not be for sale but I will keep it for myself."

So, the man went and sold everything he had, including all of his pearls. Then he bought the special pearl he had found, and he was happier than ever before in his life.

Jesus was using the story to explain that God's kingdom

142

is worth more than anything else in this world. It is the most precious treasure we can ever find. It is worth selling, or giving up, everything we have. Just like the man sold everything to get the precious pearl he suddenly found.

74. The Lost Son Comes Home

Luke 15:11-32

Jesus told a story about being lost and found. It was about a wealthy man who had two grown up sons. The younger son wanted to leave his father and his home. He wanted to go someplace far away to have a lot of fun and enjoy life on his own.

The younger son then said, "Father, you promised to give me part of your money someday. Let me have it now so I can leave home and live somewhere else." The father was kind and gave his son the money the son was going to inherit after he was dead. The son took the money and went far away to live his life on his own in another country.

In the beginning he made many new friends because he spent his money on them going to parties all the time. It was a sweet and easy life he had. But then, he ran out of money. When his so-called friends realized this, they left him and went out to find other friends. He was left with no help at all.

He then found a very lousy job feeding pigs. The son was so hungry he wanted to eat the food that he was giving to the pigs. He was very sad because he had nothing left and was afraid to go back to his father because he had disappointed him by leaving him and spending all the money. But then, one day the son said, "The servants who work for my father have more food than I have here in my misery. Tomorrow, I will go back home

and ask my father if I can become a servant and work for him."

So he went back to his father. When he was approaching the house, he could see his father running down the road to meet him. The kind father had been watching everyday since the son had left home to see if his son would come back home. That is why the father was so happy to see his boy again.

The father hugged and kissed his son. The boy then said, "Father, I have wasted your money and I do not deserve to be your son anymore. But can I be one of the servants here in your house?" The father answered, "No, you cannot be a servant. You are my son and I am so glad you are finally home again. We shall have a big party and celebrate that my son was lost but has come home to me again."

When Jesus told this story, people listened very carefully because this story was really about God. God is exactly like the kind father in the story. Even though we do wrong things and are spoiling our lives, we can always return to God. We will always be his children and God is always ready to receive us when we turn back to him, just like the youngest son returned to his father.

75. The Good Samaritan Neighbor

Many people came to ask Jesus questions. But some only wanted to try and trick Jesus and catch him saying something wrong or false. So, quite often Jesus answered these tricky questions by telling a story. One day some of the religious leaders in Israel came to Jesus and said, "The most important law is to love God completely and love your neighbor as yourself. But who is my neighbor?" They hoped Jesus would give them a wrong answer so they could criticize him.

Jesus then answered their question by telling the following story. A man traveled from Jerusalem to Jericho. It was a very dangerous road to travel and some robbers jumped on him, beat him up and stole all his money. They left the man lying beside the road. He was bleeding and could not walk, but the robbers did not care about him and left him to die.

Luckily, after a little while, a priest from the temple in Jerusalem came by. Surely you would expect such a man would help. But even though he

could see the man lying and bleeding the priest hurried on his way and did not stop to help this poor man.

A little later a Levite came by and saw the man. A Levite was also a type of priest working in the temple in Jerusalem helping with many practical things. Again, you really would expect a Levite who worked in God's temple to help the man who had been attacked. But he also looked the other way and did not stop either.

After a while a third man came along, riding on a donkey. This man was from Samaria. Jews disliked people from Samaria because they were not real Jews. Therefore Jews always tried to avoid people from Samaria. When he saw the bleeding man, he stopped the donkey and got off. Then he gave the man water and cleaned his wounds. Next, he took the man to a nearby town and found a place where travelers stay.

He gave money to the owner and said, "Take care of this man. I will pay whatever it costs for him to get well again." Having finished the story in this way Jesus now asked, "Tell me, which of these men acted like a good neighbor to the man who fell into the hands of robbers?" And they were forced to reply, "The one who helped him, the man from Samaria." Jesus then said, "Then you should also be kind to everyone you meet."

76. Lazarus, Wake Up!

John 11:1-44

Jesus often visited two sisters living in a town called Bethany. Their names were Martha and Mary. They also had a brother named Lazarus, and one day he became very sick. Therefore they sent a message to Jesus to come and see Lazarus and heal him. When Jesus heard that his good friend Lazarus was sick he said something strange, "He is not going to die but he is only sleeping. And I will come and wake him up when I get back to Bethany."

Some days later, Jesus came to Bethany, but Lazarus had already been dead and put in a tomb for over four days. When Martha heard Jesus was

on his way she went out to meet him and said, "Lord, if you had only been here before, Lazarus would not have died." But Jesus said, "Your brother will rise from the dead. Tell me, where has Lazarus been put to rest?"

They brought Jesus to a tomb where Lazarus had been placed. There was a big stone in front of the entrance to the tomb.

"Here is where Lazarus has been buried," they said. Then, when Jesus saw the grave where his good friend was lying dead, Jesus wept. Next, he commanded the big stone to be taken away from the entry to the tomb.

With a loud voice, Jesus shouted, "Lazarus, Lazarus, come out here!" And the dead Lazarus came walking out of the grave with pieces of white cloth which had been wrapped around his hands, feet and a white linen around his head. And Jesus said, "Take this off him and let him go." All who saw this were completely astonished to see that God had given Jesus the power to raise Lazarus from the dead.

77. Jesus and Children

Luke 18:15-17

Jesus often showed that he has a very special, loving heart for children. One day some women tried to bring their small children to Jesus. They wanted Jesus to put his hands on them and bless them. But Jesus' disciples tried to keep the children away from him because they thought Jesus was much too busy with more important things and did not have time for some small children.

But when Jesus saw the disciples trying to send the children away, he said, "No! You must not hinder these little children to come to me. I tell you this: If you are not going to be like these small children you will never understand God's kingdom. Let the little children come to me for they really belong to God." And Jesus received the children and put his hands on them and blessed them.

78. Zaccheaus Was A Little Man

A man named Zacchaeus lived in Jericho. He was working as tax collector for King Herod. No one liked the king and therefore people did not like Zacchaeus, either. Furthermore Zacchaeus often cheated people and made them pay more taxes than they owed. Then he kept the extra money for himself.

Zacchaeus was a very little man. When he heard that Jesus

was coming through Jericho he went out to the street to get to see Jesus. But Zacchaeus could not see Jesus over the people in the crowd. So he climbed up in a tall tree where he could sit and watch Jesus. Now Zacchaeus could easily see Jesus as he was approaching the tree in which he was sitting.

Surprisingly, when Jesus came to the tree he stopped, looked up and said, "Zacchaeus, come down. Today I want to eat dinner at your house." Zacchaeus quickly came down from the tree and took Jesus and the disciples to his house. Then he had a great meal prepared for them.

Zacchaeus was so happy that Jesus wanted to come and have dinner with a person like him. He knew he was a bad person, cheating people he collected tax money from. He could not understand that Jesus had come to his house and accepted him even though he was not a good person. Zacchaeus listened very carefully to Jesus' words. Then he said, "From now on I will do what is right. I'm going to give half of my money to poor people. And I will pay back anyone I have cheated." Jesus was very happy and said, "Zacchaeus, I have come to save people exactly like you."

79. A Colt for the Lord!

Matthew 21:1-11

When Jesus knew the time had come, he decided to travel to Jerusalem to celebrate Passover with his disciples. Jerusalem was high in the mountains, so the road was steep to climb. Jesus then sent two of his disciples into a small town they passed on their way and said, "Go into the town where you will see a donkey and her colt. Bring the colt to me."

When the disciples came to the village they found a donkey and her colt exactly like Jesus had said. When they took the colt, some men came and said, "Why are you taking the colt? It is not yours!" But the disciples answered, "The Lord needs the colt and he will soon bring it back again." It was Jesus who had told the disciples to answer in this way should anybody ask them. Then they brought the colt to Jesus.

80. Entering Jerusalem

Matthew 21:1-11

The disciples put their coats on the back of the colt and Jesus sat down on the coats. The disciples gathered around Jesus and they entered into Jerusalem. Word spread quickly that Jesus had come to Jerusalem and people ran from everywhere to see him. They cut leafy branches from palm trees and waved the branches like flags. People lay their coats and garments across the road before him and put other branches on the path. They celebrated Jesus' coming, hoping he would be their new king and throw out the Roman soldiers. They shouted, "Blessed is he who comes in the name of the Lord! Hosanna in the highest!"

81. A Very Special Meal

Mark 14:12-26

Jesus and the disciples celebrated the Passover together in Jerusalem.
Passover began in the days of Moses. It was a time for people to
remember how God had helped Moses and the Israelites escape from
Egypt. Jesus and his disciples therefore met in a house to celebrate
the Passover meal. During the meal Jesus took some of the bread and
thanked God for it. Then he gave bread to each of the disciples.

While they were eating, Jesus said something strange. "One of you has made an evil plan against me and is going to help my enemies." The disciples were very surprised to hear this and wondered who could do such a thing. Jesus then took a piece of bread, dipped it in some sauce and handed the bread to Judas. Then he said, "Judas, go and do what you have to do." Without saying a word, Judas got up from his seat, left the room, and went into the night. Only Jesus and Judas knew what the evil plan was about.

Later, Jesus also took a cup of the wine. He prayed and thanked God for it, and told the disciples to drink some of the wine. Jesus said, "I cannot be with you much longer and must leave you. When I am no longer here, you shall eat bread and drink wine together like this meal we are having. When you do so, remember me and everything I have taught you." Jesus said this because he knew that it was soon time for him to suffer and die in Jerusalem. But the disciples could not understand it.

82. In the Garden of Gethsemane

When they had finished the meal, Jesus and his disciples went to a garden right in the middle of Jerusalem called Gethsemane. Jesus asked the disciples to stay awake with him because he was overwhelmed with sorrow of what was going to happen soon. "Please, stay awake and pray with me this night," Jesus asked them. But the disciples were tired and fell asleep. Jesus was all alone as he went into the middle of the garden to

pray.

While Jesus was in this garden, Judas went to the Jewish leaders and told them where they could find and arrest Jesus. They sent out soldiers and Judas led them into the garden where Jesus was praying. Judas said, "There will be other men with Jesus and it is dark and difficult to see who is who. I will walk up to Jesus and kiss him." In this way the soldiers would know which man they must arrest. When Judas and the soldiers found Jesus in the garden, Judas went straight up to him and gave him a kiss on the cheek. Then, the soldiers grabbed Jesus.

But Peter had seen what was going on, and immediately he drew his sword to defend Jesus from the soldiers. Peter hit one of the soldiers and cut off his ear. But Jesus said, "No, Peter, it is not right of you to draw your sword." Instead, Jesus bent down, took the ear off the ground, and put it back on again and the soldier was unharmed. Then Jesus was taken away by the soldiers.

83. Jesus before the High Priest and Pilate

Mark 14:53-65; Mark 15:1-15

The soldiers carried Jesus to the high priest's house. There, they asked Jesus questions all night long. "This man claims to be God's Son. But it is not the truth. He is falsely claiming to be God. But he is a cheater and therefore he must face the toughest punishment. He must be put to death," they all shouted.

But the high priest could not sentence Jesus to death, so the next morning he was brought to the Roman governor named Pilate. They asked Pilate to have Jesus put to death. He could see that Jesus was a good man and had not broken any law. But everyone shouted louder and louder, "This man must die! This man must die!" Pilate could not stand the pressure and the big crowd of people. So he ordered Jesus to be taken outside of the city and put to death on a cross.

84. The Cross

Matthew 27:31-55

The soldiers had Jesus crucified outside Jerusalem. Two criminal robbers also hung on crosses, one on each side of Jesus. The sun disappeared and a great darkness came before Jesus died. Jesus said, "It is finished." Then he breathed his last breath. Jesus had died. Now, it looked as if Jesus had lived his life in vain and was killed as an innocent man. But the reason Jesus died in this way was because God had allowed it and decided it. Jesus also knew about it all the time. What really happened that day on the cross was that by his death, Jesus took on himself the punishment for all the evil people have done and still are doing. Actually, Jesus took every person's place on the cross and died for us. In doing so, Jesus took away our sins so we will not be judged by God for our misdeeds and the evil we do. Jesus was abandoned by God on the cross. He did this for us so that we shall never be left alone by God in the same way Jesus was. But for Jesus' friends, it was the saddest day in their lives. They could not see what really had happened and the meaning of why Jesus died. Why had God allowed Jesus to die? But this was going to change very soon . . .

85. Jesus Is Alive!

Mark 16:1-8; Matthew 28:1-10; John 20:1-10; Luke 24:1-12

Jesus was taken down from the cross and buried in a cave. A huge rock was placed right in front of it. But early in the morning on the third day after Jesus had been buried, suddenly there was a very bright light. A mighty angel went over to the cave and rolled away the stone from the entrance and then Jesus stepped out! He was no longer dead. He was alive again. God had brought Jesus back to life!

A little later that same morning the two disciples Peter and John, and a woman named Mary Magdalene, came to see the cave where Jesus had been buried. But when they approached, they could see that the big stone had been rolled away and Jesus was no longer there. The grave was empty! Peter went inside the cave and found Jesus' clothes lying on the stone where his dead body had been placed.

86. The Angel's Message

Luke 24:1-12

Mary also entered and went inside the cave. When she entered, she saw two angels. One of them said to her, "Why are you looking for Jesus here? Jesus is no longer here. He has risen from the dead and is alive again just like he told you." Mary believed what the angel said and she was no longer sad. She knew Jesus was alive. Then she went back to tell everybody the wonderful news.

Later that day in the evening, while the disciples were together in a house, Jesus came into the room. They talked with Jesus and they also touched him. Now they were no longer sad, but full of joy and happiness as they had seen Jesus and now knew for sure he was alive. Jesus also showed himself after his death to many other people at various times and locations. All people who met Jesus were sure that he was now alive again and that God had raised him from the dead.

87. The Big Catch of Fish

John 21:1-12

One night not long after Jesus had died and been brought back to life again by God, the disciples went out fishing. They had fished all night, but they didn't catch any fish and now the sun began to rise. A man was walking along the shore. He called to them and said, "Drop your net on the other side of the boat. That is where the fish are."

For some reason without really knowing why and who the man was, the disciples obeyed and dropped the net into the water on the other side of the boat. When they pulled up the net again, it was heavy with fish. It was truly a miracle! John then said to Peter, "I am sure that must be Jesus!"

Immediately, Peter jumped into the water and swam to the shore. He was so excited that he could not wait to see Jesus and talk to him. So he jumped into the sea with all his clothes on to get to Jesus as fast as possible. The others came behind him in the boat dragging the heavy nets full of fish.

Yes, it was Jesus. He was sitting

calmly by a fire and was cooking fish, for his friends the disciples. "Would you like some breakfast?" he asked them. Jesus wanted to spend some time with the disciples. He wanted to teach them more about God and the meaning of all that had happened during this first Easter when Jesus had died and come to life again. But first of all, Jesus just wanted to take good care of his friends and make sure they were not hungry.

88. Jesus Leaves Earth

When Jesus knew it was time to leave earth, he took his disciples to a hill outside of Jerusalem. Jesus said, "It's time for me to go back to heaven to be with my Father. After I'm back in heaven, you must go back to Jerusalem and wait there until I will send my Spirit upon you. After that you will go out everywhere in the world to tell people about me and everything I have taught you during these years we have spent together."

When Jesus had spoken these words, he began to rise from the earth and went up and up until a cloud covered him as he went out of sight.

For a long time, the disciples stood silent and looked up into the sky. They did not know what to think and say about this. Jesus had gone back to heaven to be with God.

As the disciples stood and looked up in the sky, suddenly, two angels stood

beside them. They said, "Why are you standing here looking up in the sky? Jesus has gone to heaven and one day Jesus will come back to earth again the same way you have now seen him leave earth." So the disciples returned to Jerusalem and stayed there waiting for God's Holy Spirit to be sent to them just like Jesus had promised.

89. Flames of Fire

One day, the disciples were gathered at one place in Jerusalem close to the big temple. The temple was filled with people because it was a very special Jewish holiday. Every year Jews from all over the world traveled to Jerusalem to celebrate this holiday in the temple.

Suddenly there was a loud noise. It sounded like a mighty wind. And a small flame of fire appeared above each of the disciples' heads. This was the gift Jesus had promised the disciples when he left the earth. It was God's Holy Spirit which now came upon them. This was the sign for the disciples that it was time for them to start telling people about Jesus.

People rushed over to see what was going on. They were very surprised. For now they could hear the disciples speak about Jesus and God in their own language. People had come from many countries, each one speaking their own language. But now, they all could hear the disciples speak to them in their own language. God had given the disciples very special powers this day so they were suddenly able to speak in languages they had never learned. People were completely amazed.

90. Peter and John in the Temple

Acts 3:1-10

Another day, the two good friends, Peter and John, were on their way up to the temple to pray and tell about Jesus. Right outside the entrance to the temple they saw a man who could not walk. He always sat just outside of the temple begging people for money so that he could buy food and clothes. He had been begging since he was a child.

When Peter and John came by, the man looked at them and asked them for some money. Peter and John stopped, looked at him and felt sorry for him. Peter then said, "We don't have silver or gold. But we will be most happy to give you what we have. In Jesus' name I say to you: Stand up and start walking!" And Peter took the man's hand and helped him up on his feet.

Immediately, an amazing power rushed through the man

and he felt strength in his legs once again. Now he could walk and jump. Dancing and singing, he went into the temple to praise and thank God for healing him through Peter.

Peter then said, "It is Jesus' power which has healed the man." And all the people who had just seen the fantastic miracle with their own eyes were completely amazed about what God had done. So they all started to praise and thank God because the lame man could walk again.

91. When Saul Became Paul

Acts 9:1-19

After the disciples had received God's Holy Spirit, more and more people became followers of Jesus. Or as we say today: Christians. The church grew very fast. But it was not easy at all to be a Christian. Many of the disciples and the first Christians were being caught and put into jail. Especially, one man in Jerusalem named Saul did not like Christians at all.

Saul was a well educated man and came from a good family. He was also a Roman citizen. But he hated Christians deeply. So he went up to the rulers and said, "Let me hunt down these people who say they believe in Jesus. Let me have them arrested and put away." The rulers gave Saul permission to do so. Therefore, he spent a lot of time traveling from city to city catching Christians and putting them in jail.

Saul went to many towns looking for Christians to catch them and have them arrested. One trip took him to a city named Damascus. When he heard that there were many Christians in this city, he wanted to get there to split up the churches, catch the leaders and put them to jail. It was far from Jerusalem so it took him several days to walk there.

92. On the Road to Damascus

Acts 9:1-19

Something completely changed Saul's plans completely on his way to Damascus. He had almost reached the city when suddenly a bright light began to shine on him. The light came from the sky and it was so bright that Saul could not see or keep his eyes opened. Saul fell to the ground and realized the light had left him blind.

Just then a voice spoke to him and it said, "Saul, why are you fighting Me?" Saul was shocked and asked, "Who are you?" And the voice said, "I am Jesus." Jesus then told Saul to go into the city and wait there. Later Saul would understand what he had to do.

Saul's friends guided him into the city because he was still blind. They took him by the hand and led him to a house in the city. Saul stayed in this house and prayed for three days and nights. Then God sent an old man named Ananias to talk to

Saul. Ananias touched Saul's eyes and all at once he was able to see again. Ananias also explained that God wanted Saul to be a leader in the church. God wanted Saul to spend the rest of his life following him and teaching others about Jesus.

That same day Saul was baptized. Because he was now a Christian he also changed his name to Paul. He changed name to make it clear to everyone that he had now started out a new life as Christian. Paul spent the rest of his life traveling to many places. He told everyone he met Jesus and what it means to be a Christian. The man who once had caught and put the Christians in jail now became one of the leaders of the churches. During Paul's lifetime, thousands of people in many parts of the world became Christians because of what he shared with them about Jesus.

93. Paul in Prison

Acts 16:16-34

It was not easy at all for Paul to become a Christian. He had many enemies who lied about him, beat him up and did all kinds of evil things to him. Paul was also put in prison many times. One night, he and a good friend named Silas had been thrown in prison. But even in the prison, Paul and Silas continued to tell about God, and they were singing about him and praying in their prison cell.

It was around midnight, and Paul and Silas were still singing. Suddenly, a mighty earthquake struck the prison. The thick prison walls began to shake and all the doors came open so it was possible for all the prisoners to escape. Paul and Silas also had a chance to escape, but all the prisoners stayed where they were.

Now, the man in charge of the prison was very afraid. If anyone escaped, he was responsible and would be punished. Maybe he would even be put to death because the prisoners had escaped. But Paul called out to the man and said, "Don't worry, everyone is still here. No one has escaped."

The man rushed into the prison cells. He looked around and just as Paul said, no one was gone. This prison leader knew that Paul and Silas believed in Jesus. He had heard them, as they were singing and praying. Then he said to Paul, "I want to be a Christian. Can you tell me more about it?" He then brought Peter and Silas from the prison to his home. His wife gave them something to eat and Paul baptized him and his whole family. Now they were Christians too.

94. Paul's Sea Travel

Acts 24-28

Paul had once again been put in prison and this time he was kept to stay there several years. Then Paul was reminded that it was possible for him to complain over his arrest to the Emperor in Rome. This was possible because Paul was a Roman citizen. Therefore, the soldiers put Paul on a ship that was scheduled to sail to Rome. Some of Paul's friends also came along on this long boat journey.

In the beginning the weather was nice and the sea was calm. But then the wind became stronger and stronger and it was difficult for the captain to steer the boat. Paul warned the captain and said, "Don't go any further. We will all die if you continue." But the captain and the soldiers decided to continue, not seeking harbor.

95. Shipwrecked!

Acts 24-28

Right after this decision a mighty, strong storm came and hit the ship with big waves. The ship was rolling forth and back and all the sailors were afraid the ship would sink. They had absolutely no control over the ship. For three days the ship was caught in the storm and everyone began losing hope they would survive and see land again.

Paul then called on everyone and said, "You should have listened to my warning, but don't give up hope now. God has told me that we all will survive and reach land, and I trust in God." The next morning the weather was much better and the wind not so strong. They gained control over the ship, and now they also could see land, so they set course toward the shore.

But just as they set sails, the ship ran aground. The big waves began to hit and tear the ship apart, so everyone had to leave before it sank. The soldiers considered killing the prisoners before leaving, but they decided to give everyone a fair chance to swim and reach the shore. Those who could not swim grabbed on to some wood from the ship. And just like God had promised Paul, all of the 250 men who were on board the ship reached the shore and were saved.

96. Paul in Rome

Acts 24-28

After the shipwreck Paul and all the men on the boat reached to an island called Malta. They had arrived on the island when a poisonous snake bit Paul. Everybody thought that Paul was going to die though he had just been saved from shipwreck. But Paul just shook his arm and the snake fell of. God protected Paul and nothing happened and Paul did not die from

the snake bite. Paul and his travel companions had to stay on the island for over three months until a new ship came and brought them to Rome. Finally, after a very long and dangerous journey, Paul arrived in Rome, the world biggest city.

Paul was watched by guards in a house waiting for his trial. But the guards were kind to him and so he still had many chances to tell the people he met Jesus. People from all over the world came to Rome, so the message of Jesus spread quickly throughout the world. Paul also had many Christians visiting him in Rome and he shared all he had learned about God.

Paul also wrote many letters to churches. God gave Paul the words to write. Paul wrote about how to live as Christians. He wrote about serving God and loving others, about marriage and about how to live right in the eyes of God. The letters were never destroyed but kept safe by the leaders in the churches. This is also why we today still can read in Paul's letters in our Bible.

97. Letters to the Churches

Paul wrote many letters to the churches. But Jesus' two disciples, Peter and John, also wrote many letters to different churches all over the world. They wrote letters to teach other Christians about Jesus, his life, death and resurrection and about God and his love. These letters were really appreciated by the Christians. Every time they gathered in church, they took these letters and read them over and over again.

98. John on Patmos

The disciple John had been one of Jesus' closest friends. He lived longer than any other of the disciples and became a very old man. He spent all his life telling about Jesus and he traveled to far away countries to do so. But late in his life, John was arrested and forced to stay all alone on a small island called, Patmos. He was there in a prison. In this way, people hoped he would not be able to continue to speak about Jesus anymore. But it did not go that way. Because now John had plenty of time to write long letters to the churches. He gave the churches many good advises and encouragement through words John received from God. God also gave him a vision of what was going to happen in the future and he wrote about everything in a long letter which was sent to seven different churches.

99. Heaven

One day John had a very special experience. Suddenly, he could see right into heaven, where God is. He could see Jesus dressed in a splendid white robe and he saw God's throne surrounded by a rainbow. From the throne came flashes of lightning, rumblings and peals of thunder. All around it he could see angels and they were singing, "Holy, Holy, Holy is God the Almighty. You are worthy, our Lord and God, to receive glory and honor and power, for you created all things, and by your will they were created and have their being."

Later some of the angels showed John what was going to happen in the future. John wrote down all of what he saw and was told. Then he sent letters to his friends so they could also share it with other Christians what John had seen and been told about the future.

100. God's Wonderful City

Revelation 21

John was looking into heaven and there was a very special city. It was the most beautiful city he had ever seen and everything was covered with gold and pearls. John saw the city where God and Jesus live. Even the streets were made of gold. In the middle of the city was a beautiful river and along the river were trees. The most wonderful fruits were growing on these trees and when people eat the fruit they will live forever. It is a place where there is no more pain, suffering, sickness and death. Only good and wonderful things will happen there. Jesus is waiting for us to be with him when we leave this world. He is preparing a home for us and there is plenty of room for all. It will be our eternal home where we shall live with Jesus and God forever.